A SIMPLE GOVERNMENT

Mike Huckabee served as lieutenant governor of Arkansas from 1993 to 1996 and as governor from 1996 to 2007. After coming in second place in the 2008 Republican presidential primaries, he became the host of the popular talk show *Huckabee* on Fox News Channel (where he plays bass guitar with the house band) and *The Huckabee Report*, heard on over 600 radio stations across the nation. He's also the chairman of HuckPAC, a grassroots conservative organization. His books include the *New York Times* bestsellers *Do the Right Thing* and *A Simple Christmas* as well as *Quit Digging Your Grave with a Knife and Fork*. He and his wife, Janet, have been married for thirty-eight years and have three grown children, one grandchild, and one on the way.

www.mikehuckabee.com

Also by Mike Huckabee

A Simple Christmas

Do the Right Thing

Character Makes a Difference

From Hope to Higher Ground

Quit Digging Your Grave with a Knife and Fork

MIKE HUCKABEE

A Simple Government

Twelve Things

We *Really* Need

from Washington

(and a Trillion

That We Don't!)

SENTINEL

SENTINEL

Published by the Penguin Group

Penguin Group (USA) Inc., 375 Hudson Street, New York, New York 10014, U.S.A.
Penguin Group (Canada), 90 Eglinton Avenue East, Suite 700, Toronto, Ontario, Canada M4P 2Y3
(a division of Pearson Penguin Canada Inc.)
Penguin Books Ltd, 80 Strand, London WC2R 0RL, England
Penguin Ireland, 25 St. Stephen's Green, Dublin 2, Ireland (a division of Penguin Books Ltd)
Penguin Books Australia Ltd, 250 Camberwell Road, Camberwell, Victoria 3124, Australia
(a division of Pearson Australia Group Pty Ltd)
Penguin Books India Pvt Ltd, 11 Community Centre, Panchsheel Park,
New Delhi — 110 017, India
Penguin Group (NZ), 67 Apollo Drive, Rosedale, Auckland 0632, New Zealand
(a division of Pearson New Zealand Ltd)
Penguin Books (South Africa) (Pty) Ltd, 24 Sturdee Avenue,
Rosebank, Johannesburg 2196, South Africa

Penguin Books Ltd, Registered Offices: 80 Strand, London WC2R 0RL, England

First published in the United States of America by Sentinel, a member of Penguin Group (USA) Inc.
2011
This paperback edition with a new preface published 2012

10 9 8 7 6 5 4 3 2 1

Copyright © Mike Huckabee, 2011, 2012
All rights reserved

Illustrations by Daniel Lagin

THE LIBRARY OF CONGRESS HAS CATALOGED THE HARDCOVER EDITION AS FOLLOWS:
Huckabee, Mike.
    A simple government : twelve things we *really* need from Washington (and a trillion that we don't!)
/ Mike Huckabee.
      p. cm.
    Includes bibliographical references and index.
    ISBN 978-1-59523-073-7 (hc.)
    ISBN 978-1-59523-083-6 (pbk.)
    1. United States—Politics and government—2009-   2. United States—Economic policy—2009-
    3. United States—Social policy—1993-   I. Title.
    JK275.H85 2011
    320.520973—dc22   2010046774

Printed in the United States of America

ALWAYS LEARNING   PEARSON

The easiest job in the world is to criticize and condemn the political figures who actually subject themselves to the torturous process of campaigning and governing. I've been on the receiving end, and as a talk-show host for both radio and television, I've dished some out as well, although I've tried to do it honestly and even fairly.

Some of the Bronx cheers we send up to those in office are well deserved, but most of the harshest critics offer their crusty curses without having the personal courage to ever put themselves on the ballot.

While there are some absolute bums in the business, there are many very honorable people who seek office and serve faithfully for all the right reasons. It's been my distinct pleasure to work with many good and decent public servants who were Democrats, Republicans, and Independents. Many served at extraordinary personal and financial sacrifice and gave up their privacy, their schedules, and their leisure time to live a life of constant travel and time away from home and endure the pressure and pain of the political grind.

To the many good people who do more than complain, but commit; who do more than scream, but serve; who do more than oppose, but actually propose ideas; who do more than run from their statements by hiding under the cover of anonymous blogs and phone-ins to talk radio and instead run directly into the flames of political candidacy, I dedicate this book. Without those willing to endure the process of our political system, our great republic wouldn't survive.

God bless you!

Contents

Contents

Preface to the Paperback Edition

When the original hardback edition of *A Simple Government* was released, there was much speculation that I would be a candidate for president in 2012. Frankly, I thought there was a pretty good likelihood of that as well! However, the book was not designed to be a campaign tool, but an honest observation of what was wrong with an out of control federal government that was ruining the future with massive debts, reckless and irrational spending, and a failure to understand that the real underpinnings of our civilization are simpler institutions like families.

My perspective was not that of a tenured wonk in an ivory tower on a university campus, nor was it that of one who had spent his life solely in the shackles of government jobs and political power. It was my assessment based on years in private business in media and communications and the nonprofit worlds of church, community, charity, and educational endeavors. My view was solidified by fourteen years in elected office, including an almost eleven-year stint as the CEO of a state, overseeing hundreds of boards, agencies, and commissions, and negotiating with a legislature that held an 89–11 Democratic edge in my early years in office and didn't exactly love the idea of advancing my agenda. The lessons were further clarified by traveling across the nation as a candidate for president and still resonate in my current life, living in hotels and on airplanes, speaking to audiences ranging from students in large college towns to pro-life groups at fund-raising dinners in small, out of the way places that are two hours from the nearest airport.

I believe that the message of commonsense conservatism is far more urgent and relevant now than ever before. The principles discussed here transcend the stuff a good president would be made of to outline what every American—Democrat, Independent, or Republican—needs to know to get back our country back on the right track.

Simplifying government to its essential functions is not a political platform for a campaign—it's a survival guide for our constitutional form of government that is supposed to operate with the "consent of the governed." If current polls of the American public are even within miles of accuracy, then the ruling class has clearly jettisoned the notion that they are to govern with consent since a record high number of citizens believe we're headed in the wrong direction and have lost confidence in the current president and the Congress to get us back on course.

A Simple Government is rooted in Tea Party theology with a pragmatic approach to implementing it into actual law and practice through the legislative process. During my tenure as governor, navigating the troubled waters of a partisan political climate through times of both surplus and downturns, I recognized that big problems were solved only when they were fragmented into smaller and more manageable problems and when specific people were tasked with getting things done, measured as to their effectiveness, and held accountable for the results. Ultimately, I would be accountable for their results, so carefully monitoring the progress was the centerpiece of executive responsibility.

Government as we see it today has been made unnecessarily complicated not because it needs to be or because it runs better with more moving parts, but because it creates the entrenchment of power for those who build it, fund it, work in it, and rule by it. The taxpayers are the bug, government is the windshield. And it shouldn't be that way in a culture that was intentionally and originally designed to empower the people and keep the governing class subservient and small—"simple," if you will.

While it's possible you might not agree with all my conclusions or even my rationales for arriving at them, I am of the deep conviction that the message of *A Simple Government* is more urgent, more timely, and more accurate than when it was first released. I hope you will agree.

Introduction

A government big enough to give you everything you want is also big enough to take away everything you have.

—Barry Goldwater

Since Barack Obama was elected, plenty of books have been written criticizing his administration and accusing him of all sorts of things—from being a Marxist to lying about his citizenship to being a Muslim. But if you know me or if you're familiar with my commentaries on TV and radio, you know that I don't like to make politics personal. That's because I was raised to believe in the Golden Rule, and I don't know about you, but I certainly don't like being called names or ridiculed. So I want to start out by saying that if you've come here looking for a personal attack on President Obama and those in Washington, you should head to another shelf in the bookstore.

I don't doubt for a moment that Barack Obama loves our country and wants to make it better. In my political career, I've found that to be true, more often than not, about people who take a position different from mine. Respect and civility go a long way in campaigns and governance.

That being said, I have never been afraid to criticize a person when I think it's appropriate, especially when it comes to those who run our country. I believe that every American has a right and a responsibility to speak up when they're unhappy with the way our government is run, and that's why I'm writing this book. Because as much as I respect President Obama as a human being, I can't help but think that just about everything he thinks is good for America is actually bad for our present and worse for our future.

You are probably reading this book in February 2011, but thanks to the practical demands of publishing, I'm actually writing it in the fall of 2010. As I sit here, our country is mired in a crisis that has grown progressively (no pun intended) worse since Obama entered the White House. Our national unemployment rate is stuck at around 10 percent; our budget deficit is spiraling to unprecedented levels; we've adopted a federal health-care system that promises to raise costs and worsen care, even though most Americans didn't want it in the first place. On top of all that, we face threats from abroad in the form of terrorism, illegal and out-of-control immigration, and two wars (though allegedly the war in Iraq is over) that we can't seem to win. Meanwhile, our image abroad is rapidly sinking to where it was during the Carter years, as we've turned our backs on some of our most trusted international allies, like Israel, in favor of "diplomatic relations" with enemies like Russia and Iran.

We were promised better than this. The election of 2008 was supposed to signal the arrival of a "postpartisan" presidency. Happy days! Joy to the world! Well, did that happen? Candidate Obama said he would discover common ground between the two major parties and come up with public-policy answers that both sides could consider viable. Instead, President Obama has shown himself to be the *most* partisan president in my lifetime, hands down. In this respect, he has far outdistanced any political gamesmanship ever practiced by any president before him, whether Democrat or Republican. Bright as he seems to be, he consistently mistakes his election for a mandate to compromise our nation's future with breathtakingly sweeping plans like socialized medicine and so-called financial reform. And make no mistake about this: Those schemes and others have already saddled our descendants for generations with a mountain of debt that they can never pay back. (I'll have more to say about this later, with the scary numbers to prove it.)

In our political tradition, as you know, it's business as usual for candidates to campaign with harsh words for the opposition. The problem comes when the bickering continues after the swearing in. A true leader's Job One is to bring people together, not just mouth partisan slogans, and as hard as it may be to believe in our increasingly partisan world, I've known people on both sides of the aisle who have exhibited such character. One of those people is former president and fellow Arkansan Bill Clinton. Even though he strenuously campaigned for every opponent I ever had in Arkansas—whether I was running for U.S. senator, lieutenant governor, or governor—not once did he stoop to personal attacks or snarky comments about my being a Republican. He treated his opponents with respect and civility.

Well, I guess these are different times. But my biggest problem with President Obama isn't his insistent partisanship; it's his reliance on advice from people who don't understand the real world that you and I live in. Obama has overloaded his administration with policy wonks and Ivy League professors because he speaks their language. Virtually no one on his team has had experience running anything; they probably couldn't even run a lemonade stand. Their abstract theories, airy platitudes, and unrealistic promises may sound nice on paper or in a congressional debate, but in reality these politicians are just trying to cover up their own ignorance.

You don't need the wisdom of Solomon to see that their lack of experience is the reason we're currently experiencing an economic crisis. Think about it. When you're a governor or mayor—or even a small-business owner—you don't have the option of printing money to cover your mistakes or to buy things you can't afford. I know. In Arkansas I had to balance the budget the old-fashioned way: The money coming into the state coffers had to be greater than or at least equal to the money going out. The result? Sometimes hard choices had to be made, but I made them. As those great political philosophers the Rolling Stones said, you can't always get what you want.

We have to hold the federal government to the same standard, and not only on the budget. On this and other issues there is a strong and building urgency to repair our weakened nation and rebuild the confidence of the American people. We need to go back to the first principles that the Founders built into our amazing Constitution. That means, in part, that we need decisive action now, not professorial dialogue and insanely complicated schemes that kowtow to special interests (like the three thousand pages of the ObamaCare bill).

In short, we need a government that works for the people. We need a simple government.

Don't get me wrong: I know that many of the nation's problems are highly complex. But I also know that the governing principles that can solve them, if we work together, are simple. Justice, integrity, freedom—the basic notions upon which America was founded—are simple. Somewhere along the way, too many of our leaders have picked up the idea that it takes something like rocket science or brain surgery to deal with public problems. Wrong. When a new law is too long for anyone to read, let alone understand, it's too long, period!

I've tried to follow the same principle in writing this book. First, I've approached the various topics here with the *simple* underlying principles that helped make our country strong. Then, in each case, I've explored solutions that would be consistent with those bedrock ideals.

I'm not trying to win a Pulitzer Prize or impress the folks at Harvard, Yale, or Stanford—if they'd even listen to me! I'm writing directly to everyone who loves America and believes that it's still the greatest country in the world (and can become even greater once we get back to basics) despite today's serious challenges. I'm writing for people who aren't ashamed to eat hot dogs and hamburgers (in moderation!) and probably think that a meal of snails is better suited to birds and fish than to humans.

Simply put, in other words, this book is intended for about 80 percent of the American people. And if just half of that group would read it and take it to heart, my wife and I would be set for quite a few of the golden years! But more important, my readers would be empowered and energized to restore clarity and common sense to our national government, just as the Founders intended.

Along the way, I hope to tell you some things you've probably never heard and remind you of some important things you may have forgotten, while keeping it all entertaining enough that you won't fall asleep midparagraph.

I also promise to be honest—perhaps painfully and brutally honest, when necessary. My goal is to be clear and open, and if that offends some people I'm all right with that. Personally, I'm so sick of the hypocritical, cynical, uninformed nonsense I've read and heard lately that I'd prefer to risk having some readers hate this book because they *did* understand it rather than have many hate it because they *didn't* understand it.

Of course, what I really hope is that, because you do understand the book, you'll *love* it. Call me vain if you want, but I think you're going to!

Mike Huckabee
October 2010

CHAPTER ONE

The Most Important Form of Government
Is a Father, a Mother, and Children

We Need a Return to Family Values

There's an old Japanese proverb that says, "It is easier to rule a kingdom than to regulate a family." I don't know who said this, but as someone who's done both (though I'd hardly call Arkansas a kingdom), I can say with absolute certainty that he was right.

I'll bet you've never thought of your family as a government. But when you get right down to it, it's the form of government that matters most—much more than Congress, or your state legislature, or even your neighborhood block association. Get your family right, and its strength will wind its way up to the highest levels of global power. Of course, the reverse is also true: When the family fails, so do the other organizing structures around it.

Why does a person commit a heinous crime—use a deadly weapon to rob someone, vandalize a school, rape a woman, murder a hapless victim for twenty dollars, or steal millions from investors (perhaps including friends and relatives) in a Ponzi scheme? Are these acts caused by incomprehensible wickedness? Are these people just plain bad? No, it's really very simple. These are people who failed to grasp—or were

7

never offered—the simplest lessons of self-discipline, respect for others, and a strong sense of human decency. And where should those lessons be taught and learned? It's not the job of a school, a workplace, or even a church to provide these most basic of life lessons (though we shouldn't forget about them there either). And besides, even when we do rely on institutions for these lessons, they usually fail.

No, these lessons cannot be taught by a teacher, boss, or minister. In order to create truly valuable and respectful citizens, these lessons need to be taught at home. By the time we enter school or start a job, we should have learned how to behave. I'm not usually a pessimist, as you probably know, but I'm afraid that if a child has not learned to behave by age four or so, he or she never will.

When I was a child and did something my mother found objectionable, she'd say, with some exasperation, "Were you raised by wolves?" Of course (being objectionable), my immediate inclination was to whip back a smart-aleck answer like "No, ma'am. I got it from you!" But I never did because I knew that the wolf in her would come out and probably chew me out. Plus, I knew what she meant: This was her way of reminding me that I was supposed to try to achieve a certain level of civil behavior. I might even demonstrate a notable difference from animals in the wild by using a napkin, saying a blessing before diving into a plate of food, or washing up before sitting down to eat. Such civilized rules of courtesy, kindness, and unselfishness were expected of me not merely so that I could get what I wanted but because, quite simply, they were *right*.

To this day, I try to behave the way my mother wanted me to—not because I'm afraid of being grounded (my wife does that now) but because she taught me the difference between right and wrong and showed me by example how to behave. These principles originate, of course, from the family.

Okay, let me say it before you do: No family is perfect, and even children raised in wonderful families can turn out to be like wolves.

Still, it makes sense that children nurtured with rules are far more likely to follow them than those given free rein to follow their most primal instincts of "self first, others second." In the national ongoing conversation about how to change "government" and make "society" better, I rarely hear a reference to the obvious starting place: the creation and nurturing of functioning families, in which a mother and a father bring up their offspring with the understanding that the older generation is training the younger to be their replacements.

This essential belief is not (at least it shouldn't be) a partisan issue, but sometimes it can seem like one. For example, President Obama, speaking to the West Point graduating class on May 22, 2010, said, "American innovation must be the foundation of American power." Yes, innovation is important (as I will discuss in later chapters of this book), but, to repeat, I believe that the foundation of American power has always been and must continue to be . . . (drum roll, please!) . . . the American family.

On this issue, as on so many others, I cast my lot with Ronald Reagan, who said, "The family has always been the cornerstone of American society. Our families nurture, preserve, and pass on to each succeeding generation the values we share and cherish, values that are the foundation of our freedom."

It should surprise no one—certainly it would not have surprised President Reagan—that those who now want to "transform" traditional America recognize this truth from the opposite direction and have placed the American family smack in the crosshairs. You know this. You see it every day. The family structure that made this country the most powerful and prosperous in the history of the world—father, mother, children—is under assault today as never before.

As parents and even grandparents, what can we do? Simple. We fight back. What happens in our day to the traditional family will determine whether we remain a morally healthy nation of self-reliant families, for the most part, or degenerate into a decadent welfare state of shattered, chaotic, and dependent families.

If you think I'm exaggerating, a little history lesson might be in order. (Many of us somehow managed to get a high school diploma even with a meager knowledge of history, but I digress. . . .) In 1917, when the communists seized power in Russia, they immediately and frankly set out to destroy what they saw as the two biggest threats to their authority: religion and the family. According to an article in the July 1926 issue of *Atlantic Monthly*, the Bolsheviks hated the institution of the family with a fierce passion. They forbade all religious ceremonies, which had the effect of turning marriage into just a piece of paper issued by a clerk. In turn, marriage could be undone in a matter of minutes by a piece of paper from another clerk. The ultimate aim of this new socialist state, so far as family was concerned, was to promulgate free love. Along the same lines, abortions were officially sanctioned and paid for by the government.

The article contained some startling facts to back up the report:

> It was not an unusual occurrence for a boy of twenty to have had three or four wives, or for a girl of the same age to have had three or four abortions. Some men have twenty wives, living a week with one, a month with another. . . . They have children with all of them, and these children are thrown on the street for lack of support.

The party's long-term goal? To throw families into chaos, thus making children loyal to the state rather than to their parents. To that end, children still living at home were told to keep a close eye on their parents and, if they criticized the regime, turn them in to the authorities. So now the young, after all, knew better than the old!

Almost one hundred years later, of course, the Soviet Union has collapsed. We don't live in the shadow of the cold war; but threats lurk elsewhere. The legacies of this massive failed "experiment" are the ideas of sexual revolution that live on and wreak havoc in our own society today through legalized abortions (and the movement in favor of having them funded by the government), seemingly casual divorce (for the first time, in 2010 fewer than 50 percent of American adults were married), growing nonchalance about unwed pregnancy among teens, and, finally, the fevered attempts to extend the definition of marriage beyond "one man, one woman." Not even the heirs of Marx and Lenin thought of going that far!

Pull Up the Drawbridge

From our friends across the pond, the Brits, we long ago adopted the idea that "a man's home is his castle." Fine, so far as that goes, but we must remember this: Castles were built not as mansions or showcases to impress the neighbors but as fortresses that would provide protection from ruthless enemies. Not to sound paranoid (just realistic), but I believe that in America today, as in the Russia of 1917, the family has lots of enemies—not all of them clearly identifying themselves or riding up armed and mounted on a steed. So parents really do need to draw up the drawbridge against a widespread culture of vulgarity and violence. You don't have a drawbridge? That's fine, because you have something better—parental guidance. If you can monitor the influence the world has on your kids and fulfill your parental responsibility by acting as the filter representing traditional values, then you will be, in effect, keeping out any enemies threatening to take over your family.

When it comes to questionable influences, just where do you draw the line? Well, you could start with a simple premise about what's beaming in on the airwaves: Much of it deserves to land squarely in the moat. But some stuff is worse than other stuff.

Not to give government a pass here (we'll get to them), but I'd argue that pop music is often the worst culprit, with "reality TV" (talk about untruth in advertising) running a close second. Without parental guidance, an impressionable girl might learn that the way to succeed is to shed her innocence as early as possible. That means, for starters, that becoming recognized in the public eye as a talented young woman involves seminudity, plastic surgery, and maybe even a stripper pole. Also, posting naked pictures or a sex video on the Internet is a guarantee of instant attention.

This is, to some extent, just a contemporary exaggeration and exploitation of the old story of the teen years. Many girls, particularly those who don't have a dad at home, believe that male approval in the form of a boyfriend is essential to existence. I don't think any sane person who doesn't live under a boulder would try to argue otherwise. Some boys sense this very well (hello!), pressuring girls to "get with the program." One good message that did come out of feminism—that girls can write their own program instead of just trying to please boys—is now out the window among many young people, especially when dealing with their peers.

Okay, so you're fully aware of all of these influences, and you're standing warily at the drawbridge. Or maybe by now you're up on the battlements armed with cauldrons of boiling oil. Next step, aside from insisting that your home conform to your values: You have to be vigilant about what goes on in your local schools. That means get out the catapult! To be effective, your reach needs to extend as far as it possibly can.

Here are some things you might want to look into. Is your first grader reading about Dick and Jane getting a puppy named Spot, or is he learning how nice it is that Heather has two mommies? Is your eighth grader studying the fruit and vegetable exports of South American farmlands, or is he practicing how to put a condom on a banana? Or is your child not learning anything at all today after being sent home for wearing an American flag T-shirt on Cinco de Mayo—or any other day?

Don't hesitate to pore over your kids' assigned books and lesson plans. Do the history books teach them that America should be cherished—or blamed for something? Talk with your kids about what goes on in the classroom: Do any teachers preach according to personal agendas that conflict with what you teach at home? Encourage your kids to read widely for themselves, rather than be bound by the assignments from school. Help them understand that they go to school to be educated, not indoctrinated. Class is supposed to be for exercising the mind. That means they need to be taught *how* to think, not *what* to think.

Pull Up Some Chairs Around the Table

Perhaps by this point you think I'm being too optimistic. But I'm also realistic. I know from talking with parents that many are about ready to throw in the towel. They try and try again but don't feel able to counter the peer pressure and insidious media messages that bombard their kids every day. Many have come to believe that they may be fighting a losing battle. The struggle is just too difficult and exhausting.

Well, I get that. But how hard is it to have dinner with your children?

Let me share with you an amazing statistic discovered by the National Center on Addiction and Substance Abuse (CASA) at Columbia University. For the past decade and a half, researchers there have been totting up the differences between teens who eat dinner with their parents "frequently" (defined as being at least five nights a week) and those who do it only three times weekly or less. The results of a CASA report published in 2009 were dramatic:

1. Teens who eat dinner infrequently with their families are *twice* as likely to use tobacco and marijuana as those who have family dinners "frequently."

2. Similarly, they're one and a half times more likely to use alcohol.

3. And they're one and a half times more likely to get mostly *C*s or lower in school. (No one's saying that infrequent family dinners necessarily *cause* bad grades, but there's clearly some sort of correlation. Try it!)

"The magic of the family dinner comes not from the food on the plate but from who's at the table and what's happening there," explains Elizabeth Planet, CASA's vice president. "The emotional and social benefits that come from family dinners are priceless."

That means the food doesn't have to be fancy, or organic, or even homemade. What counts, evidently, is the time spent together around the table. Good grades; avoidance of tobacco, alcohol, and drugs; closer and warmer family relationships—it's a scientific fact (not to mention plain old common sense) that something as simple as sharing take-out pizza is associated with all of them!

Whatever Happened to Dad?

I've been criticized many times for talking so much about "social issues" when the *real* issue now, according to some people, is the economy. Well, buckle up, Turbo, because here's a simple, inarguable fact: Every broken, fatherless family has a tremendous economic impact.

Common sense is clear: The more families can do for themselves, the less they will need from the government. But what happens when there's no dad in the picture?

Here's what Robert Rector, a senior fellow at the Heritage Foundation, has to say about that:

> The disappearance of marriage in low-income communities is the predominant cause of child poverty in the U.S. today. If poor single mothers were married to the fathers of their children, two-thirds of them would not be poor. . . . When liberals refuse to talk about marriage and the poor in the same breath, they are guilty of willful neglect of the major source of poverty.

Surprise. Liberals are just fine with that, since one of their goals seems to be getting as many people as possible on public assistance.

According to the National Fatherhood Initiative, about one in three American kids lives in a home without a dad on the premises. Are you—like me—stunned to hear that? Allowing for exceptions, as in all things, the typical portrait of these children is grim indeed. These kids are five times more likely to live in poverty than kids living with both parents. They have higher rates of delinquency, alcohol and drug abuse, smoking, and obesity. It gets worse. They have a 125 percent higher risk of suffering from abuse and are twice as likely to drop out of school. You can guess the next stat: Girls raised by a single mother are more likely as teenagers to become pregnant themselves.

Some of you may be inclined to turn away, as if none of this has anything to do with you and your family. In fact, far from affecting only the children directly involved, fatherless families affect all of us and our descendants. The so-called dad deficit added more than $300 billion to the national deficit in 2010 because of welfare payments to moms. Many of these men are responsible—at least, in the biological sense—for two or *more* single-parent families. Remember Russia in 1917? This is exactly the same problem that the communist regime deliberately created.

Again, a relevant comment from Robert Rector: "[L]iberal politicians . . . have a vested interest in the growth of the welfare state, and nothing grows the welfare state like the disappearance of marriage." And what happens then? The bigger the welfare state grows, the more powerful it becomes. Beware a government bearing gifts, because every one of them comes with strings attached. Over time, those strings grow into heavy chains.

Basically, the decline of the family is a failure of personal responsibility. The personal rights of each one of us are sacred, a part of our connection to God, but they are linked to our personal responsibilities. If we fail to live up to those responsibilities, we will lose our rights. And the state, following its own agenda, will take over.

The Worst of Both Worlds: Out-of-Wedlock Birth and Abortion

If we could hop into our "way-back machine" and travel to Washington in 1965, we might find a young Daniel Patrick Moynihan, then working at the Department of Labor in his presenatorial days, prepared to issue a report about the rate of out-of-wedlock births among African Americans. He is clearly dismayed to report that it's almost 25 percent. Now let's zip forward again to 2008 for the latest statistics then: almost 75 percent, or exactly the reverse of the 1965 ratio of illegitimate-to-legitimate births! I can hear Senator Moynihan now from beyond the grave, intoning, "I *told* you it was getting bad. . . ."

There's more bad news from 2008. Among whites, out-of-wedlock births were almost 29 percent, higher than the rate among blacks back when Moynihan sounded his alarm. Moreover, at 41 percent, the overall out-of-wedlock birthrate for all Americans was the highest ever, compared with just 5 percent in 1960. So it's safe to say that *every* group is moving dramatically in the wrong direction.

What to do? Well, when we compare out-of-wedlock births by state, those with higher incomes and education levels show lower rates. Some observers, as you might imagine, infer that this statistic suggests a socioeconomic problem that can be solved by helping more teens stay in school so that they can go on to college and higher-paying jobs. But wait: It's not quite so elementary, my dear Watson.

Let's look more closely at the situation. While red states do indeed have more out-of-wedlock babies, the blue states have—perhaps you've already guessed it—more abortions. In fact, pregnancy rates do not differ all that much; it's abortion rates that do. As compiled by the Guttmacher Institute (using 2005 statistics, the most recent available), the abortion rate is 6 percent in Mississippi and Utah and 9 percent in Arkansas. But it's 24 percent in Connecticut, 30 percent in New Jersey, and 33 percent in New York. Shockingly, the nation as a whole aborts about 1.2 million babies each year. So no matter what you may have read or heard elsewhere (perhaps from abortion activists), higher education and income levels are not stopping young women from getting pregnant: They're just turning to a different "solution." Of course, my view is that abortion, rather than actually providing a solution, is instead an even more awful problem.

So while we should be disturbed by the huge number of out-of-wedlock births, we should be even more disturbed that abortions are so common. As hard as it can be to grow up without a dad, there's a far worse fate: not growing up at all because one's life was snuffed out in the womb.

Abstinence for Kids Is the True Freedom

It is clear to me that these two epidemics—out-of-wedlock births and on-demand abortions—are sapping America's moral strength. We have two challenges. On the one hand, we need to reduce the number of pregnancies that so often lead to sad, unstable homes and eventual divorce (assuming that marriage ever had any role to play in the situation in the first place). On the other, the answer to the likelihood that children will grow up in a fatherless home is not to abort them. The strong families this country needs are always built on two shared societal beliefs: the value of marriage and the value of human life.

"Grief still treads upon the heels of pleasure," wrote English playwright William Congreve in 1693. "Married in haste, we repent at leisure." That's certainly still true all these years later, as many young people pressured to marry in response to an unplanned pregnancy will attest. But even those who decide not to marry may eventually have reason to "repent," because the other choices can be equally dismal. As a pastor, I often saw women who suffered wrenching guilt and/or depression after having an abortion or giving a baby up for adoption. I believe these women will feel their loss and anguish for the rest of their lives. As for single mothers, they typically have to interrupt their education, entrust their children to the care of strangers, and marginally support their households on a meager income. (It's then, of course, that the kindly federal government steps in to "help.")

Kids exposed to mass culture—TV, movies, music, the Internet—are incessantly told that everybody who's "cool" has sex before marriage. What's the prob? Sex is no more consequential than a handshake, dude, so "hook up" any time you want, and with anybody. After all, doing what you want, what you feel like in the moment—that's what "freedom" is, right? Too bad our culture doesn't bother to explain that it is abstinence that is the true freedom. Only abstinence ensures that our children don't have to take on adult roles before they're ready. It's only abstinence, too, that protects their options to pursue their dreams, marry the one they love at the time that's right, and feel joyful about the choices they've made *freely* along the way.

Gay Parenthood: A Social Experiment

I have often been criticized for my outspoken views on gay marriage and homosexuality, so let me be clear. I have no doubt at all that homosexual men and women love their children deeply. Just as deeply as heterosexuals love theirs.

But love alone cannot always provide what children need. If that sounds harsh, bear with me for a moment. My main concern here is that the children, most of whom are heterosexual, will not, and really cannot, get critical early-life lessons in how a heterosexual family functions successfully. In general, men and women bring different outlooks and temperaments to the task of parenting. Those male/female dynamics that make themselves evident in parenting—including even the conflicts and inconsistencies that are likely to arise—teach a child about how men and women relate to each other. In the home with two gay parents, where is that learning going to come from? It's already challenging enough to grow up, even when the parents are more conventional role models.

Of course, I'm certainly not saying that all heterosexual parents provide, or are even able to provide, a good example to their children. I know that very well from years of conversations in my pastoral study, if not from just walking through a mall. Still, I believe that we're in denial about potential problems as we see more and more homosexual couples raising families. Essentially, these are experiments to see how well children will fare in such same-sex households. It will be years before we know whether or not our little guinea pigs turn out to be good at marriage and parenthood.

Government Breakfast: A Symptom, Not a Solution

Each year, our friends in Washington decide how much to increase the budget to subsidize school breakfasts. We may disagree among ourselves on the dollar amounts, but few ask why the government is at all responsible for this program. What does it say about our society that so many parents apparently can't get it together enough to give their children a bowl of cereal and a glass of juice? It is that they just assume, after years of the practice, that it's the government's job to pay for school breakfasts? We need to look closely at this program.

After all, the government already has plenty of jobs to do—for example, fighting terrorists (sorry . . . I believe I should have written "man-made-disaster facilitators"). Feeding our kids some breakfast? Our job. Our pioneer forebears—who grew the wheat for their toast and the apples for their juice, who raised the cow for their milk—would be appalled at how pathetic many of us have become.

Let me make clear that I am in no way suggesting that we should stop school breakfasts. Having often seen firsthand the impact of poverty and hunger among American children, I know that if we did, many kids would not get breakfast at all. In a perfect world, the government wouldn't have to feed children a breakfast because their parents would be doing the job. But as you may have noticed, we don't live in a perfect world. My own church is actively involved in going beyond the government program, conducting what we call the "backpack" ministry: It ensures that kids leave school on Fridays with a backpack filled with food for the weekend. We use backpacks so that the child does not suffer the added embarrassment of being seen carrying charitable food donations home.

Result: The child has food for the weekend and returns the empty backpack to school on Monday. The government does not pay for any of this: The people of my church do. This is closer to the ideal, I think. What a family can't do, friends and neighbors can. Government is not at all in the picture. What the friends and neighbors can't do, the church does. If this model were followed all over the country, there would no longer be a need for the government to do the things it's doing—many of which add to the problem instead of solving it. I have long said, and you may have heard me say so on the air, that if all Christians in America actually gave a dime out of each dollar to help "the poor, the widows, and the orphans," we wouldn't have fifty cents of every dollar confiscated by various levels of government, which will probably mess it up.

A Tear in the Social Fabric

Winston Churchill saw the family this way: "There is no doubt that around the family and home all the greatest virtues, the most dominating virtues of human society, are created, strengthened and maintained." True, but with this one caveat: We can guard that drawbridge and provide our kids all of the moral lessons we think they need, but it's impossible to wall them off entirely from others who don't receive similar grounding. Unless society as a whole is committed to moral behavior, everything we build for our families can be destroyed in an instant.

Take the mean streets of Chicago, where dozens of children die violently every year. Typically, the only mistake they made was being "in the wrong place at the wrong time." The columnist Bob Herbert, who has written extensively about this tragedy, interviewed Ester and Eugene Stroud after their sixteen-year-old son, Isaiah, was stabbed to death on his way home after winning a dance contest. This is heartwrenching to read:

21

> Their grief, after nearly a year and a half, seemed still to be weighing on them, like a cloak that cannot be lifted. . . . Mr. Stroud, his eyes red, recalled playing chess with his son and teaching him to swim, and watching old *Godzilla* movies on television. . . . Mrs. Stroud said, " . . . Maybe this is just a mother talking, but I think the world is a little different without him.

Mr. Herbert also interviewed the Reverend Autry Phillips, who said, "We've got young people pulling out guns at 12 o'clock in the afternoon and shooting all over the place. A lot of them are angry because their daddy's not around and their mama's on crack. Who was there to teach them how to behave?"

Very simply, my friends, that's what it comes down to. When families are torn apart, our entire social fabric inevitably rips to shreds right along with them. It takes strong, united fathers and mothers to teach children how to behave. The children deserve no less.

Parents could start the lessons with their own example each morning, by the way, as they set out the cereal, juice, and milk on the breakfast table.

Social Conservatives vs. Fiscal Conservatives

You know, when fiscal conservatives try to distance themselves from conservatives, I just don't get it. (That's what I meant back on page 14 about the criticism I get for talking so much about "social issues.") After all, it's obvious, at least to me, that everything is tied together. By fighting for marriage and the traditional family, we're also fighting against poverty and crime. Without tackling it all at once, how else can we achieve our goals of smaller government and lower tax rates?

If you disagree, I'm willing to listen, but I believe that one thing leads to another. Stronger families will produce the educated workers who will be able to generate more total tax revenue. As that happens, we'll see a decline in the need for bigger government, higher spending, and larger deficits. It's a no-brainer: Local, state, and federal governments will thereby be able to reduce outlays on welfare, food stamps, house and energy assistance, health care, law enforcement, and—last, but not least—prisons.

I see this goal as a win-win for ALL conservatives. Let the liberals continue to push for a redistribution of wealth, as President Obama clearly intends. But instead, we conservatives should call for a rededication to marriage and family, with all of the societal benefits that will definitely follow.

True Self-government

Let me again stress the parallels between family and government and even church. When a corrupt leader is in office, he corrupts what he leads. This is true of a family, true of a church, true of a nation. A corrupt father will ultimately corrupt his family. A corrupt pastor will corrupt, influence, affect, and infect his church. And a corrupt elected official will infect his nation with corruption.

I like to tell a great background story to this idea from the ninth chapter of the book of Judges in the Old Testament. It's about Gideon's son Abimelech, who craved leadership and elevated stature. But he did not want to serve the people (as so many of our politicians claim they want to do); he wanted the people to serve him. At first glance, it might have seemed that he was offering a pretty good deal: If they would only consolidate power in him, he would *simplify* their lives. This "simplification" would involve taking their responsibilities upon himself (translation: he would be taking from them *for* himself). That kind of political promise is gravely dangerous.

There are two basic elements that will collapse any organization, be it a family, a business, a church, or a government. Number one: consolidating power in the hands of too few people. That ignores the warning in the classic statement that power corrupts and absolute power corrupts absolutely. Number two: a people abdicating personal responsibility in order to remove any risk to and for themselves.

Our founders were brilliant in deciding that power would be constitutionally distributed carefully among the states, leaving the federal government very limited in its boundaries. Every amendment in the Bill of Rights expressly tells the government what it is forbidden to do. Not one of them explains what the people can't do.

Just as there are the two elements that will collapse any organization, so there are two results that will predictably come from making a single leader solely responsible for the national interest without any sharing of responsibility. First, the cowardice of the people will be revealed, because they simply do not want to be held accountable. Second, the corruption of the leader will become apparent. You can count on this: When leaders want those in their charge to become more dependent rather than less so, they are definitely moving toward corruption.

Back to Abimelech's schemes: His youngest brother, Jotham, saved the day with a very clever story about three different types of trees (an olive tree, a fig tree, and a vine tree) that were offered the position of king of all trees. All rejected the idea and all, significantly, are productive bearers of fruit. But the bramble bush, a weak and pesky plant that produces nothing useful, wanted the post. Jotham's point was that the weakest, rather than the strongest, feels the urge to dominate others. But real leadership is about risk, not self-gratification. Jotham could be talking about politics today. I've often said, "If you don't like the sight of your own blood, then don't get involved in political battles; just buy a ticket and watch from the stands!" It is a full-contact sport; those of us who choose to participate all leave the field bloody, bruised, and scarred.

Further, as I've thoroughly outlined in a previous book, *Do the Right Thing*, the very best form of government is self-government. It's the goal that every honorable leader should seek to implement for his or her followers. In the family, a good parent builds independence in his or her children, not dependence. I can't imagine that a parent would feel successful if a forty-year-old child was still living at home and was unable to balance a checkbook, wash his own laundry, clean up his own room, drive himself to do errands, or responsibly find a job or income in order to pay his part of the freight. The idea of a child's remaining permanently dependent on parents is heartbreaking. By the same token, the idea of pastors' making parishioners solely dependent upon the church ministry is the antithesis of New Testament Christianity. Instead, the Scriptures make clear that the pastor's role is to equip the saints or the parishioners to do the work of ministry as individuals. A church that provides only a forum for the pastor's ideas and encourages worshippers to follow him or her without becoming directly and personally involved in some type of genuine, living ministry to others is not even close to the biblical norm of the purpose of church.

Finally, when politicians encourage people to become increasingly dependent upon them and the government programs they create, they've violated those people's sovereignty and autonomy as individuals. You will recognize this theme throughout this book, for I firmly believe that such abandonment of personal responsibility can lead to the destruction of our nation. We must be on guard: Whether we are talking about parents, pastors, or politicians, the goal should never be to create dependence on a leader or a government program; the aim should be to nurture independence that will empower and equip, not enslave.

CHAPTER TWO

The Further You Drift from Shore, the More Likely You Are to Be Lost at Sea

We Need a Return to Local Government

Let's say you get your family in order—you raise your kids to be responsible citizens, and they grow up to be responsible, civil, humane adults. Congrats! If every family in America were like yours, we'd be in great shape.

Of course, this is probably a dream (I'm fine with being called an optimist, but I'm certainly not naive), and even if we could somehow strengthen all of our families and thus reduce the poverty and the crime rate to eliminate some of the need for welfare, prisons, and law enforcement, we'd still need our government to provide a few basic things. We'd still need highways and public schools and laws and a military to make our country stable.

No American I've met would argue against these things, but we constantly seem to get mired in a debate about who's responsible. Let's look at it simply.

If you run a family, you know everyone you're responsible for governing. You know what they need, what they don't, what they want, and what they don't want. You know what you can afford and you probably know the best way to get it. What if some stranger from the next town over came to your house one day and said he would take care of running your family for you if you gave him a certain amount of your income in exchange? You would have a say in the matter, but, oh wait, he'd also be in charge of a few other families—all different from yours—who would also get a vote. Would you trust him?

My guess is you wouldn't. But this is what it's like at the federal level of government—a bunch of strangers take your tax dollars and figure out how best to put them to use. They don't know you, and they don't understand the needs of your community like you do. As a result, they set up programs and pass laws in an effort to please everyone (often pleasing no one), and you have very little say in what happens. And the bigger we allow our federal government to get, the worse the problems become.

Every time Washington enacts a new law or mandate, you can be sure that the states, the private sector, and the people are left with less control over their destinies than they had the moment before that bill was signed. Politicians get so caught up in arguing the merits of a particular provision that we don't see the overall shift in power, especially when the bills are so large that we can't deal with their totality. Power is a zero-sum game. In other words, whenever the federal government accumulates more power, the states and the people inevitably lose some autonomy they previously had. Eventually, we can lose our way entirely.

That slow and steady drift . . . drift . . . drift has been going on for a long time, but this is not how the Founding Fathers intended our country to be run. The most cursory reading of early documents from our nation's founding make it clear that the original idea was a very small federal government that basically protected our borders and made sure that within the borders we could travel and do business freely. The concept was quite unmistakable—the best government would be limited and local, because it would be closer and more accountable to the people being governed. Consider the argument James Madison presented in favor of the Constitution in Federalist Paper No. 45:

> The powers delegated by the proposed Constitution to the federal government are few and defined. Those which are to remain in the State governments are numerous and indefinite. The former will be exercised principally on external objects, as war, peace, negotiation, and foreign commerce; with which last the power of taxation will, for the most part, be connected. The powers reserved to the several States will extend to all the objects which, in the ordinary course of affairs, concern the lives, liberties, and properties of the people, and the internal order, improvement and prosperity of the State.

Madison obviously never envisioned FDR's New Deal, LBJ's Great Society, or Obama's "Fundamental Transformation." To young people today, his words must sound as though he's talking about life on another planet. I'll bet that in Madison's wildest dreams he never imagined Supreme Court decisions, like *Roe v. Wade*, that would turn the courts into a bottomless pit of federal power. We've gone so far out to sea that we've actually reversed roles, so that now it's the federal powers that are "numerous and indefinite." With the current administration at the helm, they're getting more numerous and indefinite every day!

The country Madison describes doesn't even remotely resemble the United States of the early twenty-first century. How could this happen? What can we do? Well, the first thing we must do is set a goal: to recalibrate the balance of power closer to the original Madisonian ideal.

Ronald Reagan understood this in 1981, when he declared in his first presidential inaugural address, "All of us need to be reminded that the federal government did not create the states; the states created the federal government." In his 1982 State of the Union address, he said, "Our citizens feel they've lost control of even the most basic decisions made about the essential services of government, such as schools, welfare, roads, and even garbage collection. And they're right." Reagan knew what was happening. But Reagan came and went, and the tidal pull of federal control has continued. If Reagan felt that frustrated about the expansion of federal power in 1982, imagine how he'd feel today.

Federal Money Means Federal Control

Federal aid to the states has been growing steadily since the Great Society of the 1960s, interrupted only by a decline under President Reagan. We keep hearing that the $862 billion stimulus—revised upward from the original paltry $787 billion Congress passed—didn't accomplish anything, but actually it did. In the first quarter of 2009, for the first time in our history, federal aid became the largest source of revenue for state and local governments. What a proud day! They must've been popping open the champagne in Washington when they heard that.

But at the state and local levels, it's another story. Reliance on money flowing down from the federal government, rather than up from citizens, distorts how our state and local governments function. In his 2008 article for the Heritage Foundation, "Federal Funds and State Fiscal Independence," Sven R. Larson wrote:

> Joint state-federal spending programs also increase both individual dependence on the government and states' dependence on the federal government and federal taxpayers. State fiscal policy is increasingly tied to the execution of federal spending programs and policy priorities. With this

growing dependence comes a shrinking independence in state fiscal policy, making states increasingly less able to make fiscal choices that fit their residents' needs and preferences.

In other words, money is power, and the more revenues come from the federal government, the more state and local governments will be answering to it—its priorities, its policies, its rules—before they answer to their own constituents. We find ourselves paying more and more in sales, property, and state income taxes but having less and less say in how the money is spent because of the dominant influence of federal power. This is how federal aid insidiously corrupts and destroys the proper functioning of the Tenth Amendment. Federal money is like the "free sample" of heroin that drug dealers give away. Once state officials start taking it, it leads to a spiral of dependency that requires enormous willpower to break.

One of the reasons some governors didn't want "free" stimulus money is that it was for programs they wouldn't have been able to fund once the federal money ran out. They knew that while the federal government giveth, it can also taketh away, and that makes it virtually impossible for states to plan in the long term. States didn't want to have people get hooked on new federally funded programs and then have to cancel them.

I know all too well how this game works from my own experience with the federal government during my tenure as governor of Arkansas. Whether we're talking about Medicaid, education funding, highway money tied to adherence to federal speed laws, or unemployment benefits, states are increasingly enslaved to the federal masters, and that means being held hostage to policies that may not be in the best interest of the state. To be fair, this is not a practice that happens only under Democrats—it's not that much different under Republican presidents.

Also, the federal government can be like a well-meaning relative who sends you extravagant gifts that reflect their taste, not yours. Never mind that this relative lives way beyond his means and has borrowed the money he spent on you from you! (That's another chapter.) Although America is a melting pot, we're far from a homogeneous society; life in Maine is very different from life in Mississippi or Montana. Despite Rodgers and Hammerstein's urging that "the farmer and the cowman should be friends," farming communities are different from ranching communities, which, in turn, are different from factory towns or suburban office parks.

As long as we're referencing Rodgers and Hammerstein (bet you didn't think I knew Broadway musicals), I'll go on to say we need to run from the idea of a centralized "Bali Ha'i," the symbolic utopia of everyone's hopes and dreams. That kind of place isn't real; it's a ridiculous campaign slogan. And I hope I'm not just "A Cock-Eyed Optimist" when I say our differences—social, economic, cultural, and geographic—can and should be respected and our diversity celebrated. Local residents know what they need, and it doesn't help them to have the federal government blow their grandchildren's tax money on a new airport terminal named after their senator when what they could really use is a middle-school gym and some bike paths.

You know, I have a great name for that school: James Madison Junior High.

The States as Laboratories: When Experiments Fail

Supreme Court justice Louis Brandeis, in a well-known dissenting opinion from 1932, wrote, "It is one of the happy incidents of the federal system that a single courageous state may, if its citizens choose, serve as a laboratory; and try novel social and economic experiments without risk to the rest of the country."

Brandeis had a good point, but nowadays the federal government seems to ignore logic in pursuit of its own agenda. In a real laboratory experiment, researchers start with a hypothesis and devise ways to test it; if the outcome doesn't support the outcome they'd expected, they must revise their hypothesis and subject it to more testing. This procedure is called "the scientific method." But our government is not run by dispassionate scientists.

Take ObamaCare. Ever since the debate over this program began, it's been compared to RomneyCare, the failed statewide health-care program implemented by none other than my fellow GOP member Mitt Romney when he was governor of Massachusetts. Any critical assessment of this program will show that it failed (more on this in later chapters), and yet the Obama administration decided to emulate it in its pursuit of a national health-care program. They had the facts but chose to pay attention only to the results that suited their effort to expand the federal government's control. This is not science, and it's certainly not a proper way to govern. It is pseudoscience and propaganda and an insult to our intelligence.

Justice Brandeis was right. Using states as laboratories is a wonderful idea, but if an outcome doesn't support the federal government's compulsion to expand an idea nationwide, then we shouldn't do it. We were supposed to learn from RomneyCare, not Xerox it into federal law. It is a classic example of the complete insanity of government.

The Financial Crisis and the Failure of Federalism

One of the culprits in the financial crisis that hasn't gotten enough attention is the federal Office of the Comptroller of the Currency (OCC). Not only did the OCC fail to do its job to stop banking abuses that were allowing anyone with a pulse to get a mortgage (I'm not sure that even a pulse was required), but it also kept states from regulating the mortgage madness. The rules it promulgated were so outrageous and tied the states' hands so thoroughly that the attorneys general and banking superintendents of all fifty states opposed them. Think about it—how often do all of our states agree on anything?

The rules were overturned by the Supreme Court in *Cuomo v. Clearing House Association* in June 2009, but by then we were deep in the mortgage crisis and the Great Recession. The attorney general of Idaho, Lawrence Wasden, had written in April of that year about how this failure of federalism contributed to the financial crisis:

> More than five years ago, state attorneys general warned the OCC of the problems of subprime loans. In fact, in 2003, state attorneys general traveled to Washington, D.C., to speak to the head of the OCC to warn him that lenders were pushing mortgages that were growing in risk. The attorneys general also asked the OCC for support to deal with exorbitant interest rates and fine print fees. The OCC dismissed these warnings and was steadfastly opposed to working with the attorneys general.

To expand on the observations of Attorney General Wasden, the OCC went even further to exacerbate the situation with rules that blocked state oversight of some of the financial entities that contributed to the economic crisis. In the process, it cast aside the principles of federalism on which our Constitution is based.

At a time when the mortgage-lending industry was becoming the wild, wild West, the OCC handcuffed the sheriffs—all fifty of them! We're still suffering the consequences. Again, note that these concerns preceded the election of Barack Obama and the Democrats' total control of Congress that happened after 2006. The GOP, led by the well-intentioned President George W. Bush, pushed for an "ownership society," which is laudable, but only if people *own* what they can *afford*.

I'd like to own a Falcon jet, but I don't. It's not a lack of desire but a lack of dollars!

Public Employee Unions: Another Power Grab

When California was trying to balance its budget in 2009 so that it could keep the lights on in Sacramento, it reduced payments to home health workers employed by the state. Responding to complaints from his supporters at the Service Employees International Union (SEIU), President Obama literally made a federal case out of it and forced Governor Schwarzenegger to back off that plan or lose billions from the "stimulus." It has to be more than pure coincidence that the head of the SEIU, Andy Stern, visited the White House more often than anyone else—*anyone* else—during the first half of 2009.

Let's remember that the people of California didn't elect Andy Stern to decide how their state budget should be balanced. They elected Arnold Schwarzenegger. But it seems as though both he and the residents of that state got a lesson in governing "the Chicago way."

All states except Vermont are required by their own constitutions to balance their budgets. (Vermont, given its Yankee thriftiness, does that anyway.) When states have to meet the salary, pension, and other benefit demands of public employee unions, their budgets can't stretch as far, so something else has to go. Unionized public employees cost about 30 percent more in wages and 70 percent more in benefits than those who are not in unions. They can prevent low-performing employees from being fired, as you may have seen in your child's school. They can further bloat local and state budgets by demanding that more people be hired than are really necessary to do the job, so government is more expensive and less efficient.

This keeps the states hungry for more federal money, even though it means ceding more of their power to Washington and makes them less responsive to their own citizens' preferences and priorities. In contrast, the federal government doesn't appear to be running out of money, but it certainly is. The money it's spending is Chinese. (Know the old expression "You've been shanghaied"?)

The way I see it, public employee unions have a parasitic relationship with the states but a symbiotic relationship with Washington. Here's how it works: With the force of the federal government behind them, unions get to attach themselves to the weakening states like ticks with an unquenchable thirst for power; and in doing so, they offer Washington a chance to exercise even more federal power. Both become untouchable.

It's all according to plan. Why, I can picture President Obama and Andy Stern now, walking off together through the fog, *Casablanca* style as the president says, "Andy, I think this could be the beginning of a beautiful friendship."

The BP Oil Spill: Failure to Respond to the States

If ever there was an example of the failure of the federal government to coordinate its efforts with the needs of the states, it's the BP catastrophe that happened in the spring of 2010. Day in and day out, oil poured into the Gulf of Mexico as parish, county, and state officials complained that the federal government was not incorporating their knowledge and resources effectively to align its response with their local conditions and needs. They were also frustrated by their inability to get timely approvals for their requests and answers to their questions.

As the clock ticked and the days passed, the federal government showed a maddening slowness to act—not in deference to the states (of course not) but in deference to BP—and then, once it did step in, it was dismissive of local and state officials and experts, who had a lot to offer.

There would have been less damage, both environmentally and economically, if each level of government had been able to perform the tasks it was most suited for. The role for the feds is to assist the states at the request of the governors and to make sure that a coordination of resources is taking place involving all levels of government as well as private sector resources. When it comes to oil spills, states have their own strict laws—some stricter than the federal laws—to try to protect their shores and their people. To cite just a couple of examples, California requires more intensive testing of response equipment, while Alaska requires that every tanker have two escort ships and that oil companies be able to pick up three hundred thousand barrels of oil in three days.

Billy Nungesser, president of Plaquemines Parish in Louisiana, testified before a subcommittee of the Senate Committee on Homeland Security and Governmental Affairs in June 2010, saying that he had "spent more time fighting the officials of BP and the Coast Guard than fighting the oil," and adding, "I still don't know who is in charge." With respect to Coast Guard officials who'd been charged with keeping parish officials from getting tangled in red tape, he said, "If they have the authority, they aren't using it."

The Five Levels of Government

The federal government can't seem to respect the structure of the original federalist system as set out by the Constitution, with three levels of jurisdiction: local, state, and federal. Yet when we talk about government, we really should be able to break it down into five levels: family, local, state, federal, and world.

As I discussed in chapter 1, families should have as much influence and as much power and control over all of our lives as possible. At the family level, the governing authorities (parents) are closest to the governed (children) and therefore have the deepest understanding of what is in their best interests.

At the other end of the spectrum, there's the rest of the world. Although international governing bodies like the United Nations might serve a purpose and allow us to develop relationships with other countries, it is important for America to retain its sovereignty and give faraway entities as little power and control over our lives and country as possible. I think even James Madison would agree that this is a good way to remember where power should reside—especially if he knew that terrorist nations like Libya chair the UN's Commission on Human Rights and that Iran, a brutal patriarchal regime that stones women to death for the "crime" of being raped, boasts a coveted seat on the UN Commission on the Status of Women.

At times it seems as though we've drifted so far out to sea that we'll never see dry land again. But the enduring power of our Founders in the form of the printed word—the Constitution, *The Federalist Papers*, and other writings—provides us with a sturdy anchor. And the undying yearning of Americans to live free can help us row against the tide of oppression and safely return to shore.

CHAPTER THREE

You Can't Spend What You Don't Have; You Can't Borrow What You Can't Pay Back

We Need to Control Spending and Debt

B oy, do I feel like one of the chosen people. Right this minute, there is a big smile on my face because I've just signed papers to buy a hundred-million-dollar house with sixteen bedrooms and twenty-one baths set on three hundred acres in New York's trendy Hamptons. The property comes with its own yacht dock, discreetly set-aside servants' quarters, and a twelve-car heated garage. (It can get cold sometimes at the edge of the Atlantic.) But that's just the beginning. To sweeten the deal my banker has not only approved a mortgage covering the entire amount with no collateral; he's also offered (and I accepted) an additional twenty-five million dollars for moving-in expenses. I can buy new furniture for the entire house and some really snazzy cars for the garage and hire cooks, gardeners, and a maid service to keep the whole place spotless while I watch sports on my high-definition fifty-inch flat-screen television. All of this was put together by my generous banker without a credit check or income verification, so I don't think I have to worry about paying off the loan and probably won't even bother making payments. After all, I have three kids, don't I? And grandchildren on the way? It will be their job to pay off my wife's and my debts. We raised them, so they can support us for a little while, right?

Okay, so maybe that's just a fantasy (or perhaps a nightmare). Other than the likes of Bill Gates and Warren Buffett, practically no one in America could wangle such a deal. Except, of course, the federal government. I suppose if I were the federal government, I could indeed borrow away the past, present, and future, putting completely out of my mind how on God's green earth it would be paid for. And why should I worry? Pesky details like how to pay for everything would be left to those sucker-punched Americans who aren't even born yet, won't be voting for eighteen years or more, and really won't know what hit them until they are on their own, working hard to support themselves while also paying the taxes that (let them hope) will eventually cover the cost of my excess.

Let's Do the Math

Astronomers tell us that there are as many stars in the universe as there are grains of sand on all the beaches of the world. I can't really imagine that, and I doubt you can either; in fact, the scientists themselves admit that this notion is incomprehensible even to them.

Here are two more astronomical facts. One, the federal budget for fiscal year (FY) 2011 is $3.8 trillion. Two, the ten-year budget through 2020 is $45 trillion.

It sounds like a lot, but terms like *trillion* mean little to most of us, who are used to five-figure salaries and counting quarters found in the couch cushions. *Million* sounds enormous enough; words like *billions* and *trillions* sound even more impressive. At that point, does it really even matter how many zeros there are at the end? It's still a whole lot!

Most of you have probably never seen a million dollars, let alone a trillion dollars. So for the sake of my argument, allow me to explain what this really means with a little help from the Web site Page Tutor.com.

$100

The $100 bill (what they might call "a Benjamin" in gangster movies) is currently the largest single bill in circulation in the United States. I think we're all familiar with it, though I doubt that many of us carry them around all the time.

One hundred of these bills would, of course, add up to $10,000. This amount, which would have seemed huge to my parents, is not so daunting to most Americans these days. It, or even a multiple of it, is familiar enough in any number of transactions, from taxation to tuition. But you probably don't visualize how this sum would look as actual bills. In fact, the stack would measure less than half an inch thick and could fit nicely in your pocket. Sure, it's a significant amount of money, but it's pretty easy to visualize.

$1,000,000

Let's up the ante to the next level. I'd guess that you, like most Americans, have never actually seen $1 million stacked up "in the flesh." Just look at the guy below. Next to him, the stack doesn't seem like *that* much. If you were of a mind to do so, you could readily stuff it under your mattress.

$100,000,000

Multiply by a hundred and you come up with this next stack. It's probably too hefty to fit into a suitcase, but you could stash it in the trunk of your car. And you're probably being reminded right now of news stories you've read or heard about state or even local budget items. How many of these stacks did it take to settle the new contract with the teachers' union? How many to build that new bridge or highway?

$1,000,000,000

At last we begin to reach the real money. A billion dollars sure is a whole lot, no question, but I could easily load the stacks below into the back of a U-Haul. I don't know why I would do that, but to be safe, I'd ask for an armored truck and hire a couple of armed guards to be on the lookout.

You hear the phrase "billions of dollars" tossed around all the time. So if it's $10 billion for a bit of pork in your congressional district, you can visualize ten armored U-Hauls driving from Washington to the doorstep of your local government. Hold that thought for a moment, okay? Tell me that doesn't make a striking picture.

There are a few people around the world who are actually worth billions. If you want to know who they are, there's an annual list in *Forbes* magazine. In other words, this amount, even when increased by a factor of ten, is not completely unimaginable when you look at the drawing above. Picture the oil sheik and see how many trucks are lined up beside him in your mind.

$1,000,000,000,000

But you've been hearing a lot lately about our national debt, and you haven't been hearing the word *billion*, right? When politicians, economists, and talking heads argue with one another about the national debt, the word they use is *trillion*. Actually, they use the word *trillions*.

Opposite, you can see $1 trillion stacked up in hundred-dollar bills. Compare it with the illustration above of a "mere" $1 billion. It is one thousand times as big. Holy cow! That's a lot of money. But if you remember the lesson of the day on page 40, it will take almost four of these things to get us through 2011 and forty-five of them to get us through the next decade. So we're looking at *your* money. And your grandchildren's money. And their grandchildren's money. In other words, we're looking (and, again, what you see above is only a fraction of the debt that will accumulate) at the burden that will be inherited by your descendants.

It's still unimaginable, really, but using these illustrations we can at least begin to grasp of the enormity of the debt we face. Our generation has bought that house in the Hamptons without paying for it. Actually,

to continue that analogy, we'll be buying 38,000,000 of those nice places in 2011 alone. Am I getting your attention?

It Wasn't Always This Way

It's a good thing that almost no one today pays much attention to past presidents (or even knows who the heck they are). I mean, it would really mess things up for Obama and Congress if they were to hear, much less heed, the following warning from President Eisenhower's famous farewell address on January 17, 1961:

> As we peer into society's future, we—you and I, and our government—must avoid the impulse to live only for today, plundering for our own ease and convenience the precious resources of tomorrow. We cannot mortgage the material assets of our grandchildren without risking the loss also of their political and spiritual heritage. We want democracy to survive for all generations to come, not to become the insolvent phantom of tomorrow.

Old Ike would be a real party pooper in today's Washington. For having the audacity to "pee in the punchbowl" during the never-ending frat party (otherwise known as a session of Congress), he'd be ushered off to the banks of the Potomac.

You probably know that I've struggled to lose weight and *keep* it off. Man, I'd love a world in which I could gorge on seven thousand calories a day without becoming overweight. But I can't. When you think about it, that's not so different from wanting to draw a billion-dollars-a-year paycheck while never having to show up for work, or from wanting to purchase any article or service that struck my fancy but not ever have to pay for it. Yes, that's unrealistic, of course. It's also just plain stupid. Let's see . . . I'm beginning to understand the true nature of Congress now. We have purged our communities of the really stupid class and sent them to DC! That explains why their policies are as nonsensical as eating without regard to gaining weight or using unlimited spending accounts without regard to someday paying the piper.

As Sarah Palin might say, "You betcha!"

You might have seen the really great HBO series on John Adams back in 2010. Critics and the public alike loved it. But how many of us paid close attention to the specifics of what he believed and fought for? We're willing to be entertained by a drama about his life, yet we have failed to heed his very perceptive warnings. Take this little jewel from his first State of the Union address in 1797:

> The consequences arising from the continual accumulation of public debts in other countries ought to admonish us to be careful to prevent their growth in our own. The national defense must be provided for as well as the support of Government; but both should be accomplished as much as possible by immediate taxes, and as little as possible by loans.

Yet another killjoy! Adams would never get elected in today's political climate! And I believe you know why.

Have you noticed that President Obama loves the word *unprecedented*? He has often spoken of the "unprecedented problems" he inherited from President George W. Bush. Then there are the "unprecedented opportunities" we Americans now have because *he* was elected to the White House (Sometimes when I hear President Obama speak I want to chant the Mighty Mouse theme song: "Here I come to save the day! That means Barack Obama is on the way!") A lot's going on that's "unprecedented," all right, but that is by no means a good thing. Take the *unprecedented* "greatness" of his plans to create jobs and simultaneously save the economy, the earth, and the American dream. Uh-oh. These policies actually entrenched our national debt, killed jobs, and secured a new level of power for the federal government at the expense of families and businesses. It's only fair that someone else picked up Obama's word and found a somewhat different meaning. Michael Boskin, professor of economics at Stanford and senior fellow at the Hoover Institution, wrote the following in the *Wall Street Journal* on February 12, 2010:

> The Obama 10-year budget—*unprecedented* in its spending, taxes, deficits, and accumulation of debt—is by a large margin the most risky fiscal strategy in American history.

Congratulations, Mr. President, you've done it! You've taken the country to something "unprecedented," all right. The word you're looking for is *debt*. Enduring debt. Loads of it. (I don't think he's listening.)

Do you recall those two totals I gave you at the beginning of this chapter? They bear repeating: $3.8 trillion for the 2010 budget, $45 trillion for Obama's ten-year budget. (I hope you're not getting inured to those figures. Keep reaching for the antacid.)

Did you think that maybe cutting out a few government jobs could effectively trim those horrifying totals? Stop with the Kool-Aid. This should sober you up. About 60 percent of the budget is allocated to only three things: Social Security, health-care costs (Medicare, Medicaid, SCHIP [State Children's Health Insurance Program], though mostly Medicare), and defense spending. Each makes up about 20 percent, making them roughly equal.

Then "safety net" programs—unemployment insurance, food stamps, school meals, child-care assistance, housing, welfare, et cetera—account for about 14 percent. (You can keep adding as we go along.)

Veterans' and federal retirees' benefits are around 7 percent, interest on the national debt is 6 percent, education is 3 percent, infrastructure is 3 percent, science/health research is 2 percent, nondefense international spending is 1 percent. So, if you've been paying attention, how much is left over? Something like 4 percent, which is assigned to a glob of miscellaneous expenses.

How much wiggle room is there in all this? Consider that back in 1970 the budget was designed so that a third of the total was mandatory, two-thirds discretionary. But in the early 1970s discretionary spending began growing at 5 percent annually, then jumped a whopping 27 percent from 2008 to 2009 because of increased spending on unemployment, food stamps, and the start of the various stimulus programs. In other words, the proportion of mandatory to discretionary outlays has pretty much reversed: now two-thirds mandatory, one-third discretionary.

Think about that astonishing switch: In only one generation, we've completely changed how the budget functions. In the 1970s, the largest part of the budget could be cut by Congress, because it was considered discretionary. Now only a third can be cut, because the rest is mandatory.

It gets worse. When President Obama talks about possibly freezing discretionary spending for three years, he's not focusing on even that one-third. He has his eye on only *nonsecurity* discretionary spending, or only about 15 percent of the total budget. He does not want to touch Social Security, Medicare, Medicaid, veterans' programs, defense, homeland security, or foreign aid. By that definition of *freeze*, the budget would be cut by only $250 billion over the next ten years—the proverbial drop in the bucket. Or, if you remember the illustration, the capacity of only 250 U-Haul trucks, or twenty-five a year.

There's a simple answer to this nonsense: Define *all* spending as discretionary. When so many expenditures are essentially on autopilot, driven by inflexible formulas, we the people have given up our right to representation. Moreover, our senators and congressmen have abdicated their responsibility to represent us. What sense does this make? Just as it is wrong for us to spend so irresponsibly that we enslave future generations, it is wrong to allow ourselves to continue to be enslaved by decisions made in the past.

All of us—the representatives and the represented—should agree to stop considering entitlement programs the third rail of politics—necessary and fatal if touched! The more likely fatality will occur if the emergency brake is not applied to prevent the looming crash: To activate that brake, we have to reduce the growth rate of entitlement costs.

Deficits

What's going on with the deficit flies in the face of the title of this chapter: The federal government is spending so much more than it takes in that it will never be able to make up the difference. Cue smoke and mirrors! The deficit was $162 billion in FY 2007, then leapt to $459 billion in FY 2008 before soaring to a record $1.4 trillion in FY 2009.

Originally, the FY 2010 deficit was estimated to reach $1.6 trillion. Given better-than-anticipated revenues, if the books have not been cooked, the administration brags that the deficit could actually be only (!) $1.3 trillion, assuming that the trend continues to the end of the fiscal year.

President Obama's ten-year budget, which runs through FY 2020, projects deficits that will total $10 trillion.

So what level of debt can the country afford? Put another away, what's a reasonable deficit? Economists can agree, I believe, that it should be no more than 3 percent of our annual gross domestic product (GDP). Even as recently as FY 2007, it was only 1.2 percent of GDP.

Then the economy collapsed. Since then, we've been running deficits of around 10 percent of GDP, which are very dangerous levels. Only three times before in our entire history have deficits been so high: the Civil War, World War I, and World War II.

But by 2035, according to an estimate by the nonpartisan Congressional Budget Office (CBO), deficits will reach a historic (and terrifying) high: 15 percent of GDP. Not surprisingly, given this information, a survey by the Business Council found that American CEOs believe the deficit to be the most critical policy challenge now facing the country.

Unlike a gift that keeps on giving, President Obama's misbegotten $787 billion addition to our deficit—the so-called stimulus package— is the mistake that keeps on costing. It's a shame to throw away money, even if you can afford to do so; it's dangerous when you truly, truly cannot afford it.

Nor was this response to economic crisis a sensibly targeted program to create jobs. Frankly, we could have accomplished more by just taking the $787 billion and dividing it up, like the loaves and fishes, among every American: a check in the amount of a little over $2,600 for every man, woman, and child, or over $10,000 for a family of four. Most Americans I know could certainly use $2,600 and would probably spend it. Eventually, of course, the same people who enjoyed spending it would, as taxpayers, have to pay it back. But at least they could choose how it was spent in their personal lives. Under the Obama plan, by contrast, we still have to pay it back, but the government got to decide how it would be spent. The cost of the stimulus, by the way, is not just the original outlay; you have to add the interest that we'll be paying on it for years and years to come. The government didn't find the kind of 0 percent interest deal that might still be available at your desperate local car dealer.

National Debt

Of course, these annual national deficits add to our combined national debt, which is about $13 trillion now and growing at the rate of about $4 billion every single day! That's even more than hedge fund managers make!

Our friends at the Congressional Budget Office have another grim estimate: The cost of interest on the debt will more than triple in just the next decade. In fact, President Obama is on track to add more to our national debt in his first two years than President George W. Bush did in his entire eight.

An accepted yardstick for a nation's economic health is the ratio of national debt to GDP. Economists studying national debt levels over the past two hundred years have concluded that economic growth is sharply restricted when debt is 90 percent of GDP. President Obama's projected budget will raise our debt level to 103 percent of GDP by 2015, which will be extremely threatening to our national prosperity. By comparison, both Reagan and Bush 43 left office with that ratio at 40 percent.

There are many related consequences, none of them good. For example, Moody's rating agency warns that our Treasury bonds risk losing their triple-A rating. Other countries, watching us make irresponsible economic decisions, talk about abandoning the U.S. dollar as the world's reserve currency.

As for interest rates, they are artificially low right now because of the downturn. They are predicted to go up soon, meaning that carrying our national debt is going to cost us more. And as the debt increases, the cost of interest will rise right along with it. The result: a lower GDP because of less investment.

Meanwhile, we are rightfully terrified that we now owe so much to the Chinese, but we're just as terrified that they may stop lending to us. This is a security issue as much as an economic one: How hard can President Obama push them for sanctions on renegade Iran or fairness in international trade when our huge debt to them gives them so much leverage over us? I'm thinking about ordering the Rosetta Stone course in Mandarin Chinese so I'll be prepared to talk with the bankers who will own all our currency!

Social Security

Here's a dirty little secret: Social Security was never intended to finance retirements lasting decades. When the legislation was passed in 1935, and the retirement age was set at sixty-five, life expectancy was in the late fifties for men, early sixties for women. See that? It was assumed that most people would be dead before they could qualify! No one imagined those legions of healthy, lithe retirees you see in TV ads playing golf, boating, running marathons. Today, life expectancy for average Americans has reached the late seventies, and many of us will live at least a decade or two longer. This is a blessing, especially if you're healthy, but you can no longer expect the government to support you for twenty or thirty years. The original financial calculations didn't allow for that eventuality. It's that simple.

What can be done? Well, for those already retired or close to retirement age, it's too late to change benefits. That door is closed. But it is fair to ask people in their twenties, thirties, and forties—in light of radically changed life expectancy—to plan for a different kind of future, including the responsibility to provide more for their eventual retirement. For one thing, the retirement age has to be raised. For another, the benefits will have to be adjusted downward.

There's another dirty little secret in all this (actually, most people know it but pretend otherwise). Your Social Security benefits are not funded by what you actually contributed to the system over your working years. That dissipates very quickly. No, your monthly checks come from the payroll taxes paid by younger folks still in the workforce. Back in 1950, when there were sixteen workers for every retiree, the cost was spread widely. Today, there are three workers for every retiree. There will be only two in 2025.

Even as these changes were becoming crystal clear to everyone involved, it was predicted that the Social Security system would not begin paying out more than it took in until 2016. Wrong. This happened in 2010. The unanticipated shortfall was caused by the downturn: It caused some people to choose to take early retirement, and payroll taxes fell because of widespread job losses.

As things are going now, Social Security is expected to *run out* of money by 2037. Let us pause. . . . That is only twenty-six years from now. Most of you are probably old enough to know from experience how quickly that time will pass. Where will you or your children or your grandchildren be when that happens? Let's also note that Social Security, right now, has unfounded *liabilities* of about $70 trillion. That's right. *Trillion.* (You haven't yet forgotten that illustration, have you?)

What all of this means is that we must do everything we can to delay making payments to those who are too old to have their benefits reduced. Tax incentives could encourage such people to keep working beyond retirement age, letting them keep more of what they earn. (I don't know about you and your friends, but I find that most people get bored after a few months of the "golden years" and want to work at something in order to feel useful. Rocking Chairs "R" Not Us.) Also, benefits could be made higher the longer the recipient waits past age seventy to retire; currently, they stop rising at that age. Finally, some people don't need Social Security at all. Let's offer them the option of a tax-free, lump-sum benefit payable at their death to their chosen beneficiary. This provision could delay some payments for decades.

Medicare

The picture is hardly brighter with Medicare, which is expected to become insolvent by 2017 and currently carries unfunded liabilities of about $38 trillion.

Furthermore, in order to help pay for ObamaCare, Medicare is scheduled to be cut by $500 billion over the next decade. If that kind of cut is actually made (a huge *if*), shouldn't the savings be used to extend the life of Medicare rather than to pay for this new (and widely unwanted) new entitlement?

There are potential answers readily available. For instance, we could switch to vouchers for Medicare; that way, recipients would be able to buy private insurance in the marketplace. Also, we should recognize that, just like Social Security, the Medicare program has not kept pace with the increases in life expectancy. We should raise the age of eligibility. I know that's not politically smart to say, but I promised you I would do my best to talk sense in this book! This society likes to boast that age sixty is the "new forty," because people live better and longer. Fine, so if we feel as good as we did at forty when we turn sixty, shouldn't we be able to stay active and productive by continuing to work for a few more years? That would make it even more likely that the benefits will be there waiting when we reach the age or condition when we really do need them.

We Need Jobs

Our economy has tanked precipitously, but there is a very simple way to bring it roaring back. The key is jobs. When the economy slows and unemployment rises, not only do tax revenues drop, but government spending increases because of the increased demand for safety-net items like unemployment insurance and food stamps. This means that the government is forced to spend more even as it takes in less.

But while the deficit can expand very quickly, as we've experienced, it can also contract very quickly. When people both have jobs and feel confident they will either keep them or have no trouble finding new ones, they (1) spend more (remember, 70 percent of our economy is driven by consumer spending), (2) pay more to the government, and (3) take less *from* the government.

Even if Ben Bernanke is right that we can't entirely grow our way out of the current economic mess, we must wring every last drop out of growth that we can. That means creating as many jobs as we can, and job creation requires funds for new businesses to start up and existing businesses to expand. Even though small businesses create about 70 percent of our new jobs, they have more trouble getting credit than medium-sized and big businesses. They are therefore affected more seriously by our growing deficits and debt, which soak up available capital and drive up interest rates.

According to the Kauffman Index of Entrepreneurial Activity, all of the approximately forty million *net new jobs* between 1980 and 2005 were created by firms that had been in business for only five years or less. They also found that if we take firings and layoffs into account, older companies added almost no net new jobs during the same period. Yet it's harder for small start-up businesses to get financing than it is for established companies; moreover, because of the greater risk of failure, they have to pay higher interest rates just to get off the ground. As long as the government continues nutty policies that hinder or hurt small businesses, the existing factors do not bode well for job creation.

It doesn't take Nostradamus to predict the future we're facing. As the interest on our national debt pushes interest rates for the private sector ever higher, many businesses will never get started, and others will be unable to grow to their full capacity. In other words, there is really an inverse correlation between our national deficit and our future economic growth. Unfortunately, it couldn't be simpler to understand: As interest rates rise in order to finance growing government debt, fewer and fewer new jobs can be created, and that situation in turn depresses revenues and adds to the debt, which in turn pushes interest rates up even higher.

What's the Solution?

Why not just "tax the rich"? After all, we certainly hear that a lot from the White House and from a certain side of the aisle in Congress. But we have to consider one simple fact: The top 1 percent of American taxpayers now pay more than all of those in the lowest 95 percent combined. What more can they be expected to contribute? Meanwhile, about half of us pay no taxes at all—a very unhealthy situation. Almost everyone should be contributing at least something to the pot; those who don't contribute have little reason to care about what is done with everyone else's investment.

I'd say that representation without taxation is as threatening to our national character as taxation without representation. Those who don't

pay taxes—that is, who are not pulling their weight in the community—
have no real reason not to vote for more and more government services. And that will lead to more and more dependency, making the
country more and more like a European welfare state. At times, a safety
net is essential, but it must not be used as a hammock that can lull us
into lethargy. This country was built by personal responsibility, work,
and risk taking.

Maybe you personally don't have a philosophical objection to raising taxes. But practically speaking, there is no way we can tax our way
out of the current situation. As taxes are raised, growth of the GDP
is cut, basically killing the geese that lay our golden eggs.

So what's the solution?

When you come down to it, the answer is very simple (as the title
of this chapter hints): Do not spend money that you do not have. Of
course, even the simplest idea can be extremely difficult to execute.
After all, temptation has been a human problem since Eve ate the apple
in the Garden of Eden. It was certainly enticing a few years ago, if you
were living in a modest tract home, to be assured that you could easily afford a fancier house in a more upscale neighborhood, even if, in
your heart, you suspected that you really couldn't. Too many of us, of
course, gave in to that temptation. Now that some of us have lost the
big house and have had to retreat to a tiny apartment, that tract house
looks pretty good.

Fine. You learn from mistakes; you move on and do better. You take
a second job; you go to night classes. Instead of remaining chained to
a credit card and its minimum monthly payments, you set a new goal
of putting aside a year's salary in savings. You strive, by becoming the
most conscientious and productive person in your office or plant, to be
the very last person who would be fired. As you continue honing your
job skills, you add new ones to make yourself more marketable. Working hard and working smart won't just create real prosperity for you

and your family—as opposed to the illusion of prosperity a bubble creates; they will help create real prosperity for the whole country.

Americans don't have ranks and titles, and most of us like that. Still, some of us try to distinguish ourselves from the herd by showing off our "stuff," our houses, our cars. In the run-up to this crisis, many of us probably looked at our neighbors and wondered how they could support their lavish lifestyles: How could they afford that top-of-the-line remodel, not to mention those luxury cars, private-school tuition, and trips to Hawaii and Europe? Then, as we watched their house go into foreclosure and saw them slink away, we realized the truth: They really had never been able to pay for all of those nice, shiny things. They were overleveraged big time. By using what they thought was equity in their house to buy toys, they were actually using their Visa to pay their MasterCard bill. Instead of thinking, *What's wrong with us?*, since we couldn't seem to make two plus two equal eight, as they did, many of us who did not get overextended now feel pretty darned smart. We learned that not only is material wealth less important than we thought, but it is also a trap. From the errors of the high rollers, many of us have gained new priorities; we've learned to distinguish between real needs and frivolous wants. Let's join together and promise not to forget those lessons anytime soon.

Because friends, the party really is over. We have to sober up and pay for our excesses. We are entering—as we need to—a new era of reality and responsibility for our families and our country. Already American families have shown they understand this by adjusting budgets and lifestyles. So far, not surprisingly, government doesn't get it: Our leaders are still cowering behind smoke and mirrors.

Most politicians already know everything I've shared in this chapter. The problem is not ignorance but their refusal to make choices that will be painful and politically unpopular. Everyone is aware of the coming crisis of unsustainable spending, deficits, and debt. But given the way our government functions, it's likely that nothing significant will be done until that disaster is fully upon us. Once again, just as with the bank bailouts, policy will be made in the panic mode, rather than calmly and deliberately. In other words, when our finances finally crash into the iceberg, the outcome is unlikely to reflect wisdom or fairness. Instead, it will be a matter of who can get into the lifeboats first. You know who that will be: those who have the most clout and political power, who can spare themselves pain and inflict it upon someone else.

One risk we might run is that a frightened government will just print money in order to pay off its enormous debt with cheaper dollars. That will inevitably lead to inflation, or even hyperinflation. In the 1920s, a similar decision caused people in Germany to have to buy bread with wheelbarrows full of money. If you thought that was something that only happens on the History Channel, think again. And if you've ever heard or read anything about the 1930s, you know that things did not end well. What would be a windfall—a quick and dirty way out—for the government would be an unmitigated disaster for the American people. It would also upend our whole system: The government is supposed to work for *us*, not the other way around.

Do we want to imitate Europe, where the government takes care of you in exchange for very high taxes and reduced individual opportunity? Do we want to be coddled like that, or do we instead want to remain the people of responsibility who made this country strong and free? The social spending of European countries is not hindered by a military budget like ours, which accounts for almost half the world's defense spending. Would we prefer to surrender our superpower status rather than repair Medicare and Social Security?

We built America by relying on ourselves, our families, and our neighbors—not on the federal government. To change our economic system to a European-style welfare state, we'd also have to change our culture. We'd have to abandon a heritage and a set of values that has worked well for over two hundred years, much more effectively than any other in the history of the world.

That's why resolving this crisis is not just about money, about cutting this or taxing that. Rather, it is essentially about who we are. It's about who we want our children and grandchildren to be.

CHAPTER FOUR

If You Drain the Lake, All the Fish Will Die

We Need a Simple and Fair Taxation System

I t's one of the great ironies of history that a beverage so thoroughly associated with polite culture—tea—would become a flash point in America's struggle for independence. Wars have been fought over love, treasure, territory . . . but tea? Of course, what Americans have revered as the Boston Tea Party was in truth anything but, and what you may not realize is that it wasn't actually a revolt against *high* taxes. In fact, the price of tea was actually reduced by Britain's Tea Act of 1773 in an effort to prop up the floundering East India Company, which had a monopoly on tea sales to the American colonies. London knew of Americans' passion for tea (sort of the eighteenth-century version of the near-tyrannical grip Starbucks has on us today!), so, in what you might call a corporate bailout King George style, the Tea Act reduced the taxes on the East India Company's business in an attempt to support the long-standing trade giant. But as has been our own experience with corporate bailouts, the outcome fell short of expectations.

While reducing the overall price of tea for American colonists so East India could undersell illicit tea smugglers and regain its dominance of the market, prime minister Lord North left in place the Townshend duty—a tax of three pence per pound of tea—for the sole purpose of putting a stick in the eye of colonists, who were growing increasingly hostile toward taxation without representation in Parliament. Even some members of Parliament implored the prime minister to stop poking the bear in this way, but he would have none of it. He wanted to send a message. (An important footnote here is that Lord North also knew where the revenues of the Townshend duty went—to pay the salaries of Britain's bureaucrats and administrators in the colonies. Without a paycheck, he feared they'd soon "go native.")

So the tax stayed in place, and with it the British essentially told Americans, "We'll tax you as we see fit." So on the night of December 16, 1773, colonists who'd had enough of taxation without representation boarded three East India ships docked in Boston Harbor and sent 342 chests of tea to sleep with the fishes. That was both the first time Americans showed righteous indignation and the last time anyone even thought about drinking water out of Boston Harbor!

The Bostonians didn't launch a very risky blow against the most powerful government in the world just because of high taxes. They did so because they were outraged by the idea that an out-of-touch government, worried more about supporting a bureaucracy than about supporting liberty or even fair trade, could force a trifling little tax down their throats without any say on their part. The Boston Tea Party was a protest of the notion that a government could use taxes as a means to control and manipulate, rather than a means to actually govern or administer the affairs of the state. Lord North sent his message, all right, but I suspect in hindsight that was three pence per pound he wished he'd just written off the books.

Even Taxation with Representation Ain't So Grand

Even today, fights about tax rates are proxy fights. As with the Boston Tea Party, we're not really arguing about the burden of taxes but about the burden of government. Oppressive taxes and oppressive government go hand in hand. When we talk about raising or lowering taxes, that's just code for expanding or contracting the welfare state, for increasing or decreasing dependency on the federal government. The more of our money we give to the government, the more control we cede to it and the more power it has over us.

The income tax has become the most burdensome example of this notion. The nine states without an income tax—Alaska, Florida, Nevada, New Hampshire, South Dakota, Tennessee, Texas, Washington, and Wyoming—expand much more quickly, in terms of both population and economic growth, than the states with the highest income-tax rates. But the burden isn't just in the paying of the income tax; it's in the paperwork behind the paying of the tax. According to a survey by the National Association for the Self-Employed, small businesses will have a 1,250 percent increase in paperwork for their taxes by 2012 because of expanded Form 1099 reporting requirements. The more time businesses have to spend on these forms, the less time they will have to produce or sell anything, which threatens our economic growth and job creation. Not only is the government demanding more of our money starting in 2011, when the Bush tax cuts are set to expire, but it's demanding even more of our time and energy.

And the tax code actually affects how we act—in business and in life. Veronique de Rugy of the Cato Institute elaborates:

> Changes in marginal income tax rates cause individuals
> and businesses to change their behavior. As tax rates rise,

taxpayers reduce taxable income by working less, retiring earlier, scaling back plans to start or expand businesses, moving activities to the underground economy, restructuring companies, and spending more time and money on accountants to minimize taxes. Tax rate cuts reduce such distortions and cause the tax base to expand as tax avoidance falls and the economy grows.

So not only are we taking home less money in our paychecks, but our economy is suffering under the time, cost, and energy burden placed on us by our complicated tax system. There has to be a better—a simpler—way.

Show Me the Money!

Art Laffer, an economic adviser to President Reagan and the father of supply-side economics, believes that the business profits we're seeing for 2010 are artificially inflated because of tax incentives. He says that because taxes are set to go up in 2011, companies are trying to show as much income and profit in 2010 as they possibly can. He expects profits to "tumble" in 2011 because of this shift. That's just what an economic recovery doesn't need.

Laffer believes that individuals also will shift as much income as they can to 2010. He anticipates that the rise in taxes from the expiration of the Bush tax cuts (with income, dividend, capital gains, and estate taxes all going up) will cause a "crash in tax receipts" from both individuals and businesses, causing even higher deficits and unemployment.

Scott Davis, the CEO of UPS, thinks we should encourage long-term investments (investments of five years or longer) by taxing them at a lower capital-gains rate. He understands that the rise in the capital-gains rate from 15 percent to 20 percent on January 1, 2011, and to almost 24 percent in 2013 will stunt the growth of our GDP and jobs and divert long-term investment from this country. We need to do away with the capital-gains tax, but as long as we tax capital gains, I strongly agree with Mr. Davis that we should have tiered tax rates that go down the longer you hold the investment. He points out that giving investors an incentive to keep their investments longer will create capital to grow our private sector.

Tax Cuts Are Like Fertilizer (in a Good Way!)

Presidents Coolidge, Kennedy, and Reagan didn't have a lot in common other than having "Hail to the Chief" played when they entered a room. But all three presidents understood the value of putting more money—or should I say *leaving* more money—in the pockets of working Americans. That money isn't a "gift" from the government, remember. You had to work and earn it. The example each of these leaders gave us was that tax cuts increase investment, jobs, and income and generate more revenues.

When President Coolidge cut the top rate from 70 percent to 25 percent, revenues went from $719 million in 1921 to $1.164 billion in 1927. Hey, in those days, a billion dollars was a lot of money! He also lowered the national debt by 33 percent and ran a surplus every year he was in office. "Silent Cal," as they called him, may not have said much, but in this case, actions spoke louder than words anyway.

When President Kennedy cut the top rate from 90 percent to 70 percent, revenues went from $94 billion in 1961 to $153 billion in 1968. His tax cuts led to a three-billion-dollar surplus. President Kennedy was neither a conservative nor a Republican, yet he recognized that "the soundest way to raise revenues in the long run is to cut the [income tax] rates now."

When President Reagan cut the top rate from 70 percent to 28 percent, revenues went from $517 billion in 1980 to over a trillion in 1990. When the Reagan tax cuts took effect in 1983, real growth (not just inflationary growth) jumped 7.5 percent in 1983 and 5.5 percent in 1984, after no growth in 1981 and 1982. Our GDP grew by a third during Reagan's two terms.

And the Reagan cuts didn't just benefit the rich, as some would have you believe. Americans at all income levels prospered during his presidency. From 1981 to 1989, the number of Americans making less than ten thousand dollars fell by almost 3.5 million. By 1989, 2.5 million more Americans earned upwards of $75,000 than had in 1981, and almost six million more Americans earned more than fifty thousand dollars. African Americans saw their incomes rise 11 percent under Reagan, compared to 9.8 percent for whites.

Given these examples, there's no question that it's wrong to let the Bush tax cuts expire in 2011 for high earners while we are trying to get our economy expanding again. Those earners are responsible for a great deal of the consumer spending that accounts for 70 percent of our economy—spending we need to emerge on a strong and sustainable footing from the Great Recession. Further, higher tax rates mean less money available for investment and job creation, since half of all business profits, particularly those earned by small businesses, are taxed at personal rates rather than the corporate rate.

Nicole Gelinas of the Manhattan Institute notes that newly enacted tax increases (the top tax rate going from 35 percent to 39.6 percent in 2011 and the new 3.8 percent tax on investment income of upper-income people starting in 2013 to help pay for ObamaCare) will, perversely, shift money away from the private sector, where we need it to go, while encouraging state and local governments to keep spending instead of getting their houses in order. That's because the tax increases will cause upper-income Americans to put more money in tax-exempt local and state bonds, so those entities will just keep growing. But as she points out, eventually the rich will be so squeezed that taxes will be raised for everybody.

Corporations Are Not the Enemy

Most Americans I know understand that corporations shouldn't be tax mules for the government. Corporations are like the canary in the coal mine of the U.S. economy—when they do well, it's a sign that workers will do well, and the economy thrives. However, the opposite is often just as true. Michael Boskin, who is now an economics professor at Stanford and a senior fellow at the Hoover Institution and was chairman of the Council of Economic Advisers under Bush 41, explains: "Reducing or eliminating the corporate tax would curtail numerous wasteful tax distortions, boost growth, in both the short and long run, increase America's global competitiveness, and raise future wages."

The U.S. statutory corporate tax rate is 40 percent. The *effective* corporate tax rate (when you add state corporate taxes and deduct federal tax breaks) is about 35 percent—higher than in any of the other thirty-three countries in the Organization for Economic Cooperation and Development (OECD). It's significantly higher than the *average* OECD effective rate of 19.5 percent or the average G7 effective rate of 29 percent.

In the last ten years, twenty-seven of the thirty-three other countries in the OECD have reduced their corporate tax rates by an average rate of about 7 percent. This makes that "level playing field" you always hear about when people discuss international trade a little less level. It makes us less able to compete. And as capital becomes ever more mobile, this inability to compete will just become more pronounced unless we do something about our tax rates.

To create more investments, we would be much better off reducing the corporate tax rate than making the targeted and temporary tax cuts (such as bonus depreciation) that Congress typically does. Companies and their investors need to be able to rely on tax rates, rather than hoping for special, occasional breaks at Congress's whim.

If we cut corporate taxes, companies would have less incentive to move their investments and profits overseas, foreign companies would have more incentive to invest here, and we would increase jobs, wages, and tax revenues in the process.

Raising Taxes Is Not the Answer

Data from the past sixty years have shown the close relationship between federal tax revenues and GDP. The government can raise tax rates, but it can't make revenues rise to more than about 19 percent of GDP. Kurt Hauser of the Hoover Institution first pointed out this ratio about twenty years ago, and it has remained just as true ever since. When the government predicts that it will get more revenue through higher rates, it is always wrong because it doesn't account for the ways people change their behavior and manipulate the tax code in reaction to the higher rates. When we look at the CBO's projections for the next decade, we can safely assume that its assumption of increased tax revenues from the higher rates starting in 2011 is wrong, which of course means its projections about deficits are wrong.

As of this writing, Congress is in the process of raising the tax rate on "carried interest" from the capital-gains rate (which itself is going from 15 percent to 20 percent) to as high as 38.5 percent. This is going to discourage long-term capital investment just when we should be encouraging it.

When we want to discourage a behavior, like smoking, we tax it more. Why on earth would we want to penalize long-term investment in one of America's largest industries, whether automotive or steel, now, as we are trying to get companies going and growing and Americans back to work? If you were trying to come up with a counterproductive tax increase to slow growth and kill job creation, this would be it.

This reduction in after-tax returns means money will be diverted from the partnerships that are our main source of long-term investments. Venture capital will dry up. Nothing ventured by investors, nothing gained by American workers. This change is a dangerous abandonment of our long-standing tradition of taxing long-term investments at a lower rate than short-term investments, to reward those who are willing to invest in America and wait patiently for results rather than just pursue the quick buck. It makes you wonder whose side Congress is on. Do they really prefer money going out for unemployment benefits, food stamps, and Medicaid, rather than money flowing in from more working Americans?

Why "Fair Tax" Isn't an Oxymoron

A 2008 study from the OECD found that the taxes "most harmful for growth" are corporate taxes, followed by personal income taxes. Consumption taxes are least harmful. Nobel laureate Robert Lucas believes that eliminating corporate and personal income taxes in favor of a consumption tax is "the largest genuinely true free lunch I have seen."

As many of you may know, I am a longtime supporter of the Fair-Tax. Why? The answer is in the name—it's *fair*! Imagine a world where you could chose how you spend your money—where you could choose how much tax you pay based on what you buy instead of the government deciding how much you owe based on what you earn. That's the FairTax. In a nutshell, the FairTax would levy a nationwide national sales tax while doing away with the federal income and payroll taxes, as well as estate, gift, capital-gains, self-employment, Social Security/Medicare, and corporate taxes. Beyond that, it would repeal the Sixteenth Amendment, allow Americans to take home 100 percent of their paychecks (unless they live in a state with its own income tax), and end compliance costs built in to the goods and services we buy. Not to mention, the IRS would be dismantled, as the national sales tax would largely be handled by existing state sales tax infrastructures.

Another feature of the FairTax that makes it unique is the "prebate." In order to make sure no one is taxed on the essentials of life, every registered American household would receive a monthly rebate check (prebate) to cover the sales tax on essentials up to the poverty level. This basically "un-taxes" the poor, lowers the general tax burden on most Americans, and makes the tax system progressive based on spending choices. No longer would those who are successful be penalized for their success by being stuck in a high tax bracket. They'd pay taxes commensurate with their spending choices. That's certainly not the tax code we've come to know and "love," is it? Why, it's almost fair, not to mention rather simple.

Avoiding Another Housing Bubble

Under the FairTax, people wouldn't be pushed into buying a house to get tax breaks when they'd rather rent. If there's one thing we've learned in the last two years, it's that sometimes it actually makes sense to rent. The FairTax would give Americans more freedom to live how they wish, rather than encourage them to buy houses they can't afford, as did Fannie Mae and Freddie Mac and the subprime scheme. It's also better for the government because, according to the Congressional Budget Office, all the tax breaks and subsidies for home ownership cost $230 billion in 2009. It's fairer for renters because they're not put at an unfair tax disadvantage. It's also better for those who choose to own but don't want to see their investment destroyed in a bubble.

Richard Florida, an economist from the University of Toronto, has determined that the areas that suffered the least from the housing crisis were those with the highest number of renters. The FairTax would end the distortion of the housing market, which has brutally distorted our overall economy.

Declare Those Pennies on Your Eyes

Benjamin Franklin told us the only two certainties in life are death and taxes. But there's something particularly distasteful about a "death tax."

Did you know that due to a quirk in the law, 2010 was the only time since 1916 that heirs didn't have to pay a federal inheritance tax? The reason this came about was nearly as complicated as the tax code itself. The 2001 tax-relief package passed by Congress gradually phased out the inheritance tax over ten years. But because the tax-relief bill was passed under "budget reconciliation rules," the policy couldn't extend beyond a ten-year budget window. So in 2011, the death tax—known in more polite circles as the "estate tax"—gets resuscitated, and at full 2001-level strength. Kind of like the end of a *Friday the 13th* movie— just when you think Jason's dead and the credits are about to roll, he jumps out of the lake to pull an unsuspecting victim down with him.

In 2010, we lost baseball icon George Steinbrenner, owner of the New York Yankees and (just as important to me) a recurring character on *Seinfeld*. Steinbrenner was larger than life and an astute business-man. It's estimated that his estate at the time of his death was some-where in the ballpark (excuse the pun) of $1.1 billion. If Steinbrenner had died in 2009, his heirs would have been hit with a tax bill of about $500 million. As it is, they'll still have to pay capital-gains taxes on assets should they be sold, but what will no doubt be avoided is a repeat of what happened to the Wrigley family in Chicago in the 1970s.

When Chicago Cubs owner P. K. Wrigley died in 1977, the inheri-tance tax devastated his family and forced them to sell the team to the Tribune Company in order to meet the huge tax burden on the estate.

Who knows what would have happened had George Steinbrenner's family been in a similar position?

Now, admittedly, this is a huge problem of the wealthy. But it's also a problem for the rest of us because the death tax undermines job creation. A 2003 study by economist William W. Beach found that eliminating the estate tax would create between 170,000 and 250,000 jobs. And a study conducted by Douglas Holtz-Eakin and Cameron Smith in 2009 found that full repeal of the tax would create 1.5 million jobs.

The Heritage Foundation estimates that repealing the death tax would increase small-business capital by $1.6 trillion, increase the probability of hiring by 8.6 percent, increase payrolls by 2.6 percent, and expand investment by 3 percent.

Compare the benefits of repealing the estate tax to the benefits of the $862 billion stimulus funding intended to invigorate the economy, and I think you'll agree—it's time to bury the death tax.

Something Smell Fishy to You?

In July 2010, the inflatable dam on Tempe Town Lake in Tempe, Arizona, burst, releasing almost a billion gallons of water down the usually dry Salt River bed in just a few short hours. Luckily, no one was injured in the episode . . . well, almost no one—fish casualties were high.

What was left was a stinking, muddy lake bed and shallow pools of flopping, dying fish. Crews had to stay on top of the fish problem because carrion birds see pools of flopping fish as an all-you-can-eat buffet, and the nearby Phoenix Sky Harbor International Airport couldn't have dive-bombing birds occupying its flight path. So something had to be done. Who wins in a situation like this? Well, in this case, local alligators from the Phoenix Herpetological Society, that get to feast on the stranded fish, making the circle of life complete.

This is not unlike what high taxes are doing to the American economy. Like a dam straining against the pressure of too much water, our economy is straining against the pressure of too many taxes. In 1913, when the Sixteenth Amendment was passed, less than 1 percent of Americans paid income tax and the top rate was 7 percent. In the 1950s and early 1960s, the top tax bracket was a whopping 91 percent. Even during the Clinton years, it topped out at nearly 40 percent.

If we continue to strain our economy like this, the dam will eventually burst, and all of the people who relied on that capital will be left flopping around like dead fish—at the mercy of the big bad alligator called government.

CHAPTER FIVE

Once Humpty Dumpty Falls, It's Hard to Put Him Back Together

We Need a Responsible Approach to Health and Health Care

I know all too well about the dangers and struggles of obesity. It's chased me throughout my adult life. In 2003, I lost 110 pounds and beat back early symptoms of type 2 diabetes. Since then, I have been able to live without any symptoms. As my doctor told me after I aggressively fought back with nutrition and exercise, it's as if I was never diagnosed. That's good news and I'm not taking it for granted. After a year of nonstop travel and gaining about thirty of those pounds back, I went back to a more focused lifestyle to again fight the "demon" of food addiction. It is a lifelong battle that many other Americans can relate to.

When I decided to get the thirty pounds off and get back to my marathon-running fitness, I went back and read my own book on the subject, *Quit Digging Your Grave with a Knife and Fork*. I meet people almost every day who tell me that book caused them to change their lifestyle and lose anywhere from twenty-five to two hundred pounds.

Of course, as much as I could probably flatter myself into taking credit for these people's success, I know they could never have lost the weight without taking some personal responsibility for their own health. I'm sure plenty of doctors and specialists told them, as they did me, that they would face serious health risks if they didn't take better care of themselves. But in the end, no amount of advice or warnings can make up for a lack of effort on the part of the patient.

And as much as I love hearing weight-loss success stories like these, I know that for every person who has made the commitment to eat right, exercise, and lead a healthier lifestyle, there's at least one more who still opts for the Twinkies and TV over carrots and cardio. And sooner or later, these folks end up at the doctor's office or worse, the emergency room, undergoing expensive procedures and treatments that could have been avoided with a few more good decisions.

What does this have to do with health care? It's simple, really. No matter what kind of health-care system we have, the only way to really manage costs and reduce wasteful procedures and medicines is to take some responsibility for our own health. After all, at the most funda- mental level, we don't really face a health-care crisis; we face a health crisis.

If We Can't Take Care of Ourselves, No One Can

About 75 percent of our health-care costs are from four chronic con- ditions: heart disease, cancer, diabetes, and obesity. Besides being the most expensive diseases, they are also the most preventable. These four chronic conditions are linked to four behaviors—tobacco use, alcohol use, lack of exercise, and poor diet.

In 1996, the President's Council on Physical Fitness and Sports found that almost 30 percent of our health-care costs come from lack of exercise and excess weight.

These four chronic conditions are interrelated. For example, being overweight is a cause of diabetes. Diabetes, in turn, increases your risk of heart disease (as well as your risk of kidney disease, stroke, blindness, and leg and foot amputations). But if a diabetic avoids saturated and trans fats, he can lower that increased risk of heart disease. Unless we change our ways, a shocking one-third of Americans born in 2000 will become diabetics.

Being overweight or obese increases your risk of cancer and is considered a factor in about 20 percent of cancer deaths.

Some businesses are trying to hold down health-care costs by rewarding healthy behavior through discounts on health-insurance premiums. In 2005, Safeway began its Healthy Measures plan for nonunion workers. Between 2005 and 2009, when most businesses saw their health-care costs rise almost 40 percent, Safeway's costs, amazingly, stayed the same. Safeway tests workers' tobacco use, weight, blood pressure, and cholesterol and gives employees a premium reduction for each test they pass. Steven Burd, Safeway's CEO, wrote in 2009: "By our calculation, if the nation had adopted our approach in 2005, the nation's direct health-care bill would be $550 billion less than it is today." That's a heck of a better record than *anything* Congress has passed or even proposed! Why didn't they listen to Burd? He and I both testified at a Senate hearing in 2009. I didn't expect them to listen to me in Washington, but it's a pity they didn't grasp his very compelling facts. But facts and Washington politics are like oil and water.

Besides emphasizing prevention, companies are also cutting costs through better management of chronic conditions. Boeing has reduced its health-care costs by 20 percent for employees with illnesses like diabetes and heart disease by having their doctors ride herd on them to take their medications and modify their unhealthy behaviors. Besides keeping costs down, Boeing is helping these employees enjoy the best possible quality of life despite their diseases.

While prevention is always the goal, better management of chronic conditions is also essential. Right now we have a system that happily pays for a diabetic to have his foot amputated for about thirty thousand dollars but won't pay for visits to a nutritionist or podiatrist to keep that foot healthy. That's insane.

Tipping the Scale

One-third of American adults are now obese—almost three times as many as in 1960. If we don't drop the Twinkies and pick up the carrot sticks, that number is expected to rise to almost one-half by 2020. Obesity rates are 50 percent higher for African Americans than for whites, and 20 percent higher for Hispanics, which explains why these groups suffer from an epidemic of diabetes.

Obesity-related health-care costs in 1998 were $74 billion. They are now $147 billion.

A Duke University study found that medical costs claimed from on-the-job injuries were seven times higher for obese workers.

In addition to diabetes, obesity has been linked to other chronic and degenerative diseases, like Alzheimer's. A 2010 study from Boston University School of Medicine found a link between stomach fat and a higher risk of Alzheimer's disease. Dr. Susanne Sorensen, who is in charge of research for the Alzheimer's Society, responded, "This is not really surprising as a large stomach is associated with high blood pressure, cholesterol and diabetes—all major risk factors for dementia." Is it so much of a sacrifice to go for a jog or eat a salad if it means being able to stay lucid and vital in your old age?

An Inherited Problem

Obesity is especially dangerous for pregnant women. About one in five women is obese (which means she has a body mass index, or BMI, of at least 30) when she becomes pregnant.

These mothers have much higher rates of Cesarean births, with all the risks of surgery. As BMI rises, women become two (BMI of 30–35), three (BMI of 35–40), and even four (BMI over 40) times more likely to have a Cesarean than a woman of normal weight, for whom the Cesarean rate is 11 percent.

The babies of obese mothers have double the risk of being stillborn and three times the risk of dying in their first month. They are 11 percent more likely to be born with a defective heart, and that gap jumps to 33 percent when the mother is one hundred pounds or more over a healthy weight.

These babies are less likely to be carried to term and thus more likely to need intensive (and expensive) neonatal care. A *New York Times* story about an obese woman who had a stroke and gave birth to her baby prematurely found that while a normal delivery would have cost about thirteen thousand dollars, the costs for this woman and her child were over two hundred thousand dollars!

And this problem doesn't stop with mothers. One of the most publicized interviews I've conducted for my Fox News weekend show was with First Lady Michelle Obama. Shortly after assuming the role of First Lady, she announced that she would make childhood obesity one of her major areas of focus. I was thrilled to hear it. I have taken a lot of heat from fellow conservatives who would demonize the Obamas for anything and everything, but that's absurd and as appalling as it was for yahoos like Keith Olbermann to do the same thing to President George W. Bush. We do have a serious crisis with childhood obesity in this country, and if you doubt it, here's an experiment for you. Go through your personal belongings and dig out your class photo from the third grade. The following day, pay a visit to a third-grade class somewhere in America—doesn't matter what part of the country, doesn't matter if it's a private or a public school. Walk into that class and take a look at the kids and compare them to the look of *your* third-grade class. I promise if you do this, you will never again doubt that there have been dramatic changes in the health of children in this country.

Since 1980, the number of obese children in the United States has tripled, to about 17 percent. We are seeing children as young as seven with type 2 diabetes (which used to be called adult-onset diabetes) and preteens taking medication for high blood pressure along with their grandparents. It is very sad and very scary to think that our children may have a shorter life expectancy than we do and that they will age with much illness and suffering.

A survey by C.S. Mott Children's Hospital in Ann Arbor, Michigan, found that over 40 percent of parents with obese children thought that their children were a healthy weight! We can't solve the problem if we don't recognize it.

There are more obese children in the southeastern part of the country, the so-called stroke belt. In 2010 the *Archives of Pediatrics and Adolescent Medicine* reported that Oregon has the lowest percentage of obese children and Mississippi has the highest. States where children watch more TV and are less physically active have higher obesity rates, just as you would expect.

A 2010 study from the University of Michigan found that obese children are 63 percent more likely to be bullied than thin children. Their obesity wasn't just a threat to their physical health—they also had higher rates of depression and loneliness. Even though childhood obesity has become all too common, it is still not accepted.

A study from Ohio State University in 2010 had three recommendations for reducing childhood obesity: eating dinner as a family, cutting back on TV to no more than two hours a day, and making sure that children get enough sleep.

We also need more playgrounds and walking trails, more unstructured outdoor play, more recess and physical education at school (which many schools have cut back or eliminated since No Child Left Behind), and healthier school meals, with a special emphasis on eliminating high-calorie beverages. Children should exercise for at least an hour a day, at least five days a week.

This is an issue that I've personally invested in. To be clear, I don't want the government to become "sugar sheriffs" and tell us what to eat or tax us for eating what they don't think we should eat. I do believe individuals should arm themselves with the facts and then make rational, adult decisions about their health and future. But the cost of ignoring the epidemic of childhood obesity is a staggering financial burden to taxpayers in the form of increased health-care costs for those on taxpayer-funded programs like Medicaid, as well as a body blow to the human capital that will be lost by a generation whose lives will be cut short by chronic diseases that will plague them until they die a premature death.

It's even having an impact on the military: Revelations made public in April 2010 by a panel of retired military officers showed that three out of four youths between the ages of seventeen and twenty-four were unfit for military service, primarily because of obesity!

It is crucial that we keep our children at a healthy weight, because those who are overweight or obese when they're young tend to remain so. We are setting our children up for a lifelong battle. And it's a battle that we're losing.

Take Care of Yourself

Our society suffers from a double whammy when it comes to our health. We have become more sedentary by watching TV and sitting at our computers, activities that have a symbiotic relationship with sugary and salty snacks. It's very difficult to eat a bag of chips when you're swimming or playing basketball.

An old Chinese proverb certainly applies to becoming physically fit: A journey of a thousand miles really does begin—literally and figuratively—with a single step. People say they hate exercise. But think back to when you were a child—what did you enjoy? Bike riding? Skating? Just as people who say they hate vegetables can come up with at least one they like if they think hard enough, everyone can find a physical activity that is not a chore. Start small in both time and energy expended. Take the stairs instead of the elevator; park at the opposite end of the mall from the store you're going to. Ideally, you should exercise for at least thirty minutes a day, at least five days a week.

As for losing weight, don't say, "I have to lose fifty pounds"; say, "I am going to gain my health," and when you do, take the steps to get healthy—good nutrition and realistic exercise. We all know the drill: eat smaller portions; limit high-calorie foods (those that are high in fat and refined sugar); eat more fruits, vegetables, and whole grains. But as I pointed out in my book about my own health journey, most of us need to spend a couple of weeks in "detox" from the fatty and sugary foods that we are literally addicted to.

I think it's a big mistake to set a weight-loss goal. First, to be healthy, we need to change our lifestyles, not just our waistlines. Second, Americans by nature don't want to *lose* but to *win*. If the goal is to *lose* weight, it goes against our instincts. Set a goal to *win* health, and when you take the steps to do it, weight will take care of itself.

Any amount of weight you get rid of in the process of getting healthy and keep off does you good. Your goal is to be healthier, not to be America's next top model.

A Sensible Approach to Health Care

Of course, no matter how well you take care of your body, things happen and you need to go to the doctor. And in order to stay truly healthy, you need to engage in preventive medicine as well. It is essential that we go for regular health screenings, such as mammograms and Pap tests for women, PSA tests for men, and colonoscopies and choles-terol tests for everyone. When detected early, breast, prostate, and colon cancer have survival rates of more than 90 percent. But a test can't save your life if you don't take it. Less than 40 percent of colorec-tal cancers are caught early, simply because people don't get tested. Aside from saving your life, early detection often leads to treatments that are much less grueling, debilitating, and expensive.

To do all this, we need doctors, and we need hospitals, but we need a sensible approach, and nationalized medicine is not the answer. In devising ObamaCare, the president got his priorities reversed. Rather than emphasize gaining control of spiraling health-care costs, he con-centrated on getting more people into the already flawed system. It might have had a chance to work, if he had taken the other way around. Here's how: If costs are brought under control first, then more people would be able to afford health care in the private system. Also, this ap-proach would slow the unsustainable rise we've seen in Medicare and Medicaid. Now, of the thirty million people slated to enter ObamaCare, about twenty million are coming in through an expansion of Medicaid.

Let's look at it another way. What you and I will be paying to subsi-dize other people's health care under ObamaCare could have instead been covered by cost reductions brought about by a truly free market. Instead, we get higher spending. The country is already well on the road to economic ruin (if you've been paying attention), and Medicare is on the way to rationing. ObamaCare, a huge mistake moving in the wrong direction, is foisted upon us at a critical time when eighty million baby boomers are about to enter Medicare and, in most cases, subsequently face most of their lifetime medical costs.

We should be doing several different things. We must allow health insurance to be sold across state lines—now prohibited—in order for the insured to shop around for the most reasonable policies. We need to implement legal liability reform so that personal injury lawyers can't treat the health-care system as a grab bag. But most of all, we need health insurance that is consumer based, not employer based. It's simple: You can't have a functioning free market when the person paying for the service and the person using the service are not the same. Up to now, when it comes to costs, no one has been minding the store. Because the increased costs are just taken out of wages, employers don't care. Because the employer is handling the payments, workers don't care. In fact, they may think that health care is free, but it's actually about as free as the proverbial free lunch. No such thing under the sun. Instead, it's to health care that their wage increases have gone for the last decade. Wages have not stagnated because employers aren't spending more on health care per employee; they've stagnated because those increases are going directly to the insurers, not into workers' pockets.

Right now, the working consumer—whether under a private or a government plan—pays only twelve cents on the dollar for health care. The other eighty-eight cents come from the employer. If you had to pay only twelve dollars for every $120 in groceries you bought because your boss would pay the difference, you wouldn't be reaching for the Hamburger Helper; you'd be stocking up on lobster and prime rib. Because of the present system, in other words, workers don't really have incentives to compare the relative cost and quality of physicians and hospitals or to refrain from overuse. Not every situation is an emergency. When people don't question whether or not they really need a test or procedure, it's probably because they have too little skin in the game.

Not only is ObamaCare cost prohibitive, it's already been shown to not work! In chapter 2, I mentioned how the federal government ignored the negative results of the health-care "experiment" known as RomneyCare. It could be argued that if RomneyCare were a patient, the prognosis would be dismal. "No one but Mr. Romney disagrees," quipped Joseph Rago, senior editorial writer for the *Wall Street Journal*, in a piece entitled "The Massachusetts Health-Care Train Wreck."

Governor Romney himself wrote a piece in the *Wall Street Journal* shortly after signing the bill, promising that everyone in Massachusetts "will soon have affordable health insurance and the cost of health care will be reduced." A noble goal, indeed, but when the Massachusetts Taxpayers Foundation stepped into the lab to examine this experiment-in-progress, they found that health care, which was 16 percent of the state budget in 1990, had jumped to 35 percent in 2010. (That's not a typo; health care is consuming over a third of the entire state budget!) Massachusetts spends about twenty thousand dollars to insure a family of four, while an employer-based policy costs about thirteen thousand.

You get one guess as to who now has the highest average health-insurance premiums in the country. Yep, it's Massachusetts! We hear so much flak from the administration about "unsustainable" increases nationwide in health-care costs, but according to the *Boston Globe*, premiums in Massachusetts under RomneyCare are rising 21 percent to 46 percent faster than the national average. Rather than costs being reduced, as Romney promised, everyone—government, businesses, and consumers—is paying more.

If everyone in Massachusetts is paying more, it must mean patients are receiving better care, right? In fact, just the opposite is happening. By almost three to one, Massachusetts's residents believe that the quality of their care has been reduced. The people of Massachusetts participated in an experiment that blew up in their faces, and now they have to stand in line at the burn clinic.

If our goal in health-care reform is better care at lower cost, then we should take a lesson from RomneyCare, which shows that socialized medicine *does not work*. Period. It astounds me that those on the left, claiming to advocate for those less fortunate, would push for a program that will, no doubt, put everyone in danger.

I recognize it's a tough world out there. It's scary to hear that people have lost their houses because they lacked health insurance or got dropped when they became seriously ill. I don't deny that these can be problems. But it has been less well publicized that some people lose homes *indirectly* as a result of rising health-care costs, even when they aren't dealing with a catastrophic illness. These tend to be folks who tried to make up for the stagnation in their wages by refinancing their homes on what they thought was their equity—equity that proved to be illusory and vanished in the downturn. Because what would have been their wage increases got diverted into "employer-paid" health insurance, they relied on the borrowed money to buy cars and take vacations and pay college tuition. If they had stuck with their original mortgages, which had lower balances and payments, they wouldn't have lost their homes. I think we can understand why these choices were made, even if we can agree that they did not turn out to be sensible.

When Government Plays God

When we conservatives warned that ObamaCare did not bode well for Grandma's life expectancy, we were accused of fearmongering. But nothing is more frightening than the words of President Obama's choice to head Medicare, Donald Berwick: "The decision is not whether or not we will ration care—the decision is whether we will ration with our eyes open." Funny, I never heard this among the administration's talking points when they were rounding up health-care votes in Congress. Dr. Berwick looks to Britain's socialized medicine for his inspiration: "I am romantic about the National Health Service. I love it." Uh-oh.

But we were in trouble even before ObamaCare passed. Tucked away in the $787 billion stimulus was the establishment of the Federal Coordinating Council for Comparative Effectiveness, which will become our version of Britain's National Institute for Health and Clinical Excellence, the ironically and Orwellian-named NICE. NICE decides who lives and who dies based on age and the cost of treatment. So the stimulus didn't just waste your money; it planted the seeds from which the poisonous tree of death panels will grow.

Dr. Berwick warns: "Limited resources require decisions about who will have access to care and the extent of their coverage." Yet if we were healthier, our resources would be sufficient to care for everyone.

Who will get rationed? Well, the very old and the very young, obviously, the most helpless and vulnerable among us. But it will also be those who don't live politically correct lives—those who have too many cigarettes or cocktails or cans of soda. "Death by Chocolate" won't just be a cute name on the dessert menu.

I fully realize that all health care is somewhat rationed, from the triage of the paramedics at the accident scene to the emergency room, where the most critical patients are given priority. But it's one thing for your own doctor to tell you you shouldn't have a procedure and quite another for it to be a government worker. I think I need a trip to the doctor just from thinking about giving the government that much power!

Dr. Berwick's belief system is fundamentally un-American: "The complexity and cost of healthcare delivery systems may set up a tension between what is good for the society as a whole and what is best for an individual patient." That's what happens under socialism. Individuals—your child, your parent, you—don't matter and may have to be sacrificed. By contrast, we have always believed that every life is precious; we have built the freest and most prosperous society in human history precisely by championing the individual. Americans believe that society exists to serve the individual, not the other way around.

CHAPTER SIX

If You Don't Hear the School Bell Ring, Class Never Starts

We Need an Education System That Values All Students

I love rock 'n' roll just as much as, if not more, than the next guy. One of my favorite tunes is the Pink Floyd megahit "Another Brick in the Wall": "We don't need no ed-u-cay-shun . . . Hey! Teacher! Leave those kids alone!" But as catchy as that song is, I don't think it should serve as a motto for our education system. Unfortunately, if you look around, that seems to be the case.

Case in point: A friend of mine owns a printing business, and as part of the job-application process he gives a prospective employee a ruler and a piece of paper. He tells the wannabe employee to mark one-eighth of an inch, one-sixteenth of an inch, and a few other simple measurements. He tells me that only about one in ten actually know what he's talking about!

If we are going to regain and retain our prosperity and keep America competitive in the twenty-first century, our children must get properly educated. Not only does a lack of education make children less competitive among their peers—often confining them to a life of low-paying, dead-end jobs (not to mention government handouts), but, as

Americans grow up to be less educated than their counterparts in other countries—like China and India—our nation becomes less competitive as whole.

Already we see this trend taking a toll on American jobs as large companies seek talent from abroad to fill the spaces Americans aren't skilled enough to fill. High-tech companies such as Microsoft, Google, Apple, and Cisco have had to recruit top talent from other countries such as India, Taiwan, Israel, and Japan, which have held students to higher standards in math and science while our students continue to fall behind in these areas. Our children are growing up without the basic skills they need to stay competitive in the job market. We're pushing them through a broken system and setting them up for failure on the other end.

Our children are our most valuable natural resource. The children we're educating (or not educating) today will grow up to be the presidents, business leaders, doctors, and scientists, not to mention teachers, of tomorrow. But you'd never know we were grooming such important people by the haphazard way in which we structure their education. "Book learning" needs to go a long way toward a focus on the student and not just the school. We need to ignite the innate curiosity in the minds of young people and inspire them to be lifelong learners with an insatiable appetite for knowledge and wisdom.

Yet about one-third of our students are dropping out of high school. For minorities, it's closer to 50 percent. That's more than a million students a year, or six thousand every school day. We must especially target the 12 percent of our high schools that currently produce 50 percent of our dropouts. It's hard for the student to succeed when he or she is in a school that is a dismal failure.

This is a tragedy not just for those directly involved but for our society as a whole. Considering how much we spend to put kids in school, it's a tragedy that there is such an economic impact when it simply doesn't work. A dropout can expect to earn a quarter of a million dollars less than a high school graduate, to be in worse health by the age of forty-five than a graduate at the age of sixty-five, and to die nine years younger than a graduate. Dropouts are far more likely to become involved with drugs and crime. Economists estimate that for each 1 percent rise in high school graduation rates, we'd have one hundred thousand fewer crimes every year. Considering the average cost of an inmate to be about fifty thousand dollars a year, ignorance gets *very* expensive!

Even for those who finish high school, that diploma is not what it used to be. Are the taxes you pay going to provide a high school education or a high school diploma? In too many of our schools, the two are not the same. Recognizing that a high school diploma is not what it used to be, more than half of our states have adopted exit exams designed to ensure that those receiving diplomas really deserve them. They are responding to growing evidence that our high school graduates are not adequately prepared for higher education, since one-third of those going on to four-year colleges and one-half of those going on to two-year colleges need remedial classes. This means taking high school classes at college prices, and it's costing us more than two billion dollars a year. At City College of San Francisco, a community college with one hundred thousand students, 90 percent aren't prepared for college-level English, while 70 percent aren't prepared for math.

While college enrollment keeps rising, graduation rates keep falling. Fewer than one in three students who enter a community college with the intent of getting a degree actually do so. Lack of adequate preparation is the major reason for dropping out of both two- and four-year programs.

Students who drop out of college are giving up tremendous earning potential. In 2008, the median income for workers with college degrees was almost $45,000, almost twice as much as the $25,000 median income of those with only high school diplomas.

Besides the lack of preparation for higher education, states are also facing the fact that many high school graduates can't do jobs that employers traditionally considered appropriate for them. Companies that have been burned by low-performing high school graduates are increasing their entry-level requirements to insist on a two- or four-year degree. Young people who have studied hard and done well through high school are denied opportunities where they could thrive because of the wide disparity among high school graduates.

Exit exams are a great idea for restoring the integrity of a high school diploma. Unfortunately, when the states started doing practice tests, they found that significant numbers of students failed them. You would think the states would take this as a sign that they need to smarten up their students. Instead, they are dumbing down the tests to avoid a high failure rate or putting off the testing altogether. This is not a solution; it is a sin. It's the equivalent of a basketball coach deciding that the way to help his losing team is to lower the basket from ten feet (rim to floor) down to seven feet so that every player can slam-dunk the ball. Problem is, the teams they face will be playing to the higher standard. The students from the rest of the world will increasingly be playing to a higher standard. So must we.

Lowering graduation standards is a disservice not only to our young people but also to our country. Those who receive diplomas they haven't earned may get a job, but many get fired or don't get promoted. They lack the reading comprehension and math skills they need to understand apartment leases and home mortgages; health, auto, and life insurance; and credit-card fees and terms. Besides being less equipped to care for themselves and their families, they are less able to be fully participating citizens.

I spend a lot of time at airports, and our education system reminds me of the people movers that take us between terminals. Our children get on in kindergarten and get moved along through high school. When they stumble, no one stops the conveyor belt. They just keep moving forward from one grade to the next, falling further and further behind in the knowledge and skills they need for success. It's time that our states hit the emergency button and give those who fall the practical help they need, not a phony diploma to commemorate a wasted trip.

Let's Not Flee Our Public Schools, Let's Fix Them

In Washington DC the initial group of students who won a voucher lottery to attend private school are reading two grade levels higher than those who entered the lottery but didn't win. This is a telling comparison because it shows how even the most highly motivated students and parents can't bridge the education gap without the necessary resources from our schools.

There's no doubt that the right of every citizen to a free public education is one of the things that makes America great, but our schools are still failing us. Despite the years and money spent so far on No Child Left Behind, the results of national reading tests released in May 2010 showed that inner cities are still way below the national average at both the fourth- and eighth-grade reading levels. This National Assessment of Educational Progress, nicknamed the "nation's report card," revealed that our children are severely lagging in reading comprehension skills as they enter middle school. This affects their ability to do well in just about every subject, since you can't succeed in history or science without solid reading comprehension skills.

As much as I believe education is a national problem, I want to be clear that I don't think it's best solved on the national level. As I said in chapter 2, I believe that our state and local governments are best suited to know the needs of our citizens—and that goes for our kids too. There's been a lot of talk lately about national education standards, but I do not endorse letting the federal government take over education and would oppose having it set the curriculum, standards, class sizes, or teacher pay for our public schools.

So what to do? Lately charter schools have been all the rage. A charter school differs from a public school in that, even though it receives public money and is free for students to attend, it does not operate within the normal rules and regulations of traditional public schools. Instead, each charter school draws up its own mission, or "charter," for producing results and is held accountable for achieving these results by its sponsor (e.g., a school board or state agency). Any student can apply to attend a charter school but, due to their popularity, spots are often limited and must be allocated by a random lottery system.

There are more than five thousand charter schools in the United States, with about 3 percent of our children, over 1.7 million, attending them. In some cities, that percentage is much higher, such as 57 percent in New Orleans and 36 percent in Washington DC. Much of the success of these schools depends on how much supervision they have. Charter schools in New York City have a lot of oversight and have been very successful. By contrast, in places where there is little accountability, such as Texas, Arizona, and Ohio, the charters tend not to perform very well. A 2009 study by Margaret Raymond, a fellow at Stanford University's Hoover Institution, found that 83 percent of charters did not outperform their local public schools. In fact, almost 40 percent were worse than those schools.

I support charter schools and other methods of empowering parents with choices for their students and providing competition for the existing establishment government schools. Getting more children into private schools through vouchers and scholarships and supporting high-performing charter schools are good things. But the truth is that the overwhelming majority of our children are going to go to their local public school. We have to provide solutions for them.

Our public schools have historically been outstanding, and they can be again. Instead of fleeing our public schools, let's fix them. Our schools aren't failing for lack of money. Among developed countries, we are at the top in per-pupil spending but score in the bottom third in achievement. I am a product of public schools. All three of my adult children spent their entire primary and secondary education in public schools. As much as I support and appreciate Christian schools, home-schooling, private academies, and charter schools, I doubt they will be able to replace public schools for many of America's students.

A gifted teacher can provide both the encouragement to overcome obstacles and the excitement about learning that our children need to stay in school and excel. We must attract the best possible talent to teaching. But for about the last forty years, we have been drawing from a shallower pool. We no longer have a captive, abundant supply of bright, ambitious men and women who lack other career paths. They're no longer in our classrooms—they're in our courtrooms, our operating rooms, our boardrooms. We must reestablish teaching as a respected profession, as a desirable, competitive career path, and that means abolishing tenure and providing merit pay.

The Problems with Tenure and the Promise of Merit Pay

In June 2010, Timothy Knowles, director of the University of Chicago Urban Education Institute, wrote an op-ed in the *Wall Street Journal* arguing that we must eliminate tenure for teachers:

> As a former teacher, principal and district leader . . . there are two things I've learned for certain. First, teachers

have a greater impact on student learning than any other school-based factor. Second, we will not produce excellent schools without eliminating laws and practices that guarantee teachers—regardless of their performance—jobs for life.

Most school systems follow a first-hired-last-fired rule when they have to cut back on staff. In fact, fifteen states, including large states like New York and California, have laws requiring that layoffs be based on seniority. Firings ought to be based on performance. It's a shame to keep a bad teacher because he's been there boring his students to death for twenty years and fire a gifted, inspiring teacher just because he or she arrived a year ago. Cuts should be an opportunity to get rid of deadwood, not those bearing the most fruit.

Michelle Rhee, the former chancellor of public schools for the District of Columbia, said, "When I first came here, all the adults [teachers] were fine; they all had satisfactory ratings. But only 8 percent of eighth graders were on grade level for math. How's that for an accountable system that puts the children first?"

While more than half the states offer some form of merit pay in theory, it's usually a reality in just a few districts or schools. In their 2010 paper "Blocking, Diluting, and Co-Opting Merit Pay," Stuart Buck and Jay Greene of the University of Arkansas found that of the 15,200 school districts in the United States, only 528 were using merit pay, which is 3.5 percent of districts. They discovered that where merit pay was enacted, "it often ends up being blocked, co-opted, or diluted by established interests." For example, it is enacted temporarily and then expires, or it is repealed under the excuse of budget constraints, or unions keep local districts from participating. Buck and Greene reported that of the 360 school districts in Iowa, only three applied for a merit-pay plan that was passed in 2007.

Buck and Greene wrote that merit-pay plans are foiled when pay is determined based on résumé builders like graduate degrees rather than on actual results like test scores or graduation rates. Likewise, they are ineffective when they require a very low standard of actual improvement and when they are used for what is effectively an across-the-board raise in which bonuses small and are given to most teachers.

Buck and Greene concluded that merit pay depends on school choice and competition to succeed and defeat the "powers that be":

> The problem is that public schools are not primarily educational institutions where policies are organized around maximizing student achievement. Instead, [they are] political organizations organized around the interests of their employees, their union representatives, and affiliated politicians and other interest groups—"school people instead of kid people!"

That's an interesting concept—school people versus kid people. Whom do we owe a responsibility to? Our schools or our students?

Buck and Greene went on to argue that schools should adopt merit-pay programs, which would make the teaching profession more competitive and thus attract better candidates.

Some say that merit pay wouldn't be fair, that some teachers would get more simply because the principal likes them. But isn't that how life works in the private sector? Don't some people get promoted because their boss thinks they do a good job? Merit pay at every school in the country would create a system superior overall to what we have now. We hear all this agonizing about the criteria for merit pay, about the difficulty of deciding who deserves more. The truth is that principals know who their best teachers are. Teachers themselves know who the best teachers in their school are, as do the children and their parents.

Of course, it is not easy to establish merit pay and abolish tenure.

Take Florida, where the legislature passed both reforms but they fell victim to Governor Charlie Crist's political ambitions. Having changed his party affiliation to Independent from Republican, he vetoed the bill as part of his strategy of moving leftward to try to win a Senate seat in 2010. But at the end of the day, we need to ask ourselves, who loses when we don't educate our children? Everyone.

Tough Choices for Education

During my decade as governor, there were many situations that confronted me that were not of my own choosing, and the field of education was no exception. It was always easy for some expert from out of state based at a Washington think tank to evaluate the decisions I had to make on the ground. That is the reality of leadership: Every governor in the country has to navigate whatever situation arises.

In December 2002, the Supreme Court of Arkansas finally ruled in a nearly twenty-year-old ongoing lawsuit related to school funding. The justices decided that the state had failed in terms of both educational equity and educational adequacy. The court directed the state to ensure that all students, no matter what their geographical location, be granted access to essentially the same education as all other Arkansas students. This ruling would have several consequences. For one, there would have to be increased spending on a per-pupil basis to deal with the differences in spending between affluent and less well-off communities. For another, objective evaluators would be brought in to determine exactly what was adequate and what was equitable. Arkansas schools spent considerably less per pupil than most states—in some districts, pitifully below others—so there really was no way to argue the propriety of the decision.

This was a very challenging experience. I was confronted with the necessity of getting adequate revenue to comply with the court's orders and, more important, meet the very real needs of the children of our state. But this could only be achieved if I sailed through some very unfriendly legislative waters. Nor were many people pleased when I suggested that, rather than simply spend more money, we commit to spending it efficiently. Specifically, I argued that we should not raise revenue unless we made the politically tough decision to consolidate many school districts because their separate existence could not be justified financially. Only consolidation, I felt, would produce the economies of scale that needed to be achieved in order to operate an efficient system.

In many cases, my approach was unpopular and would later provide a great deal of political fodder to my opponents in the presidential campaign. They made simplistic charges against me without putting forth any context. Of course, this is one of the most painful realities of today's politics. If a person has no record at all or, if already in political office, has carefully avoided confrontations and difficult decision making, the voter has no way of knowing what the candidate's really made of. I have always believed that ultimately, people would rather elect those with the courage to make tough decisions than those who've governed so as to preserve their own political future at the expense of a better future for coming generations.

As I've recalled for you here, in my experience, educational issues are affected by all levels of government and by the beliefs and convictions of school officials, elected representatives, and outside "experts," as well as by the legal opinions issued by courts. As I said before, education is a function of state and local governments and was never intended, as evidenced by our Constitution and the words of our Founding Fathers themselves, to be a federal concern. As we look directly into the classroom now, please don't forget this context. It is complex and can be determinative.

Race to the Top

Although I believe education should be left to the states, I fully endorse the new federal program Race to the Top, which has states compete for additional education funds, allowing them to decide what reforms to enact rather than having specific reforms imposed on them from above. Applications are evaluated under a five-hundred-point system, with points awarded based on criteria in several categories. The greatest number of points (138) is allocated to the category of reforms that address tenure and seniority.

It's a very clever way to prod states to embrace much-needed reform just out of the *hope* of getting federal money, without actually promising any particular state anything. The mere prospect of this money has motivated states to stand up to their teachers' unions or get unions to agree to reforms they've opposed in the past. It's like getting all five of your children to do a great job on their chores knowing that only the one who does best will get an allowance. For all the criticism of the Obama administration (and I've been the source of plenty), this is an area where I give them credit. If we're going to spend federal money on education and have a federal education department (even though it's not really a constitutional function of the federal government), then we ought to at least make the money count. .

The $4.3 billion allocated is less than 1 percent of the money spent annually on education by government at all levels. But small amounts of money—in fact, just the possibility of small amounts of money—can effect significant change. So far about half the states have passed reforms in their effort to get a share of this money. Forty states and the District of Columbia competed in stage one, which concluded in March 2010 with grants to Delaware and Tennessee.

Personalized Learning

Besides attracting and keeping better teachers, we have to help our teachers help our children. One of the major reasons for dropping out is simple boredom. I want to transform America's high schools by putting each student at the center of his education to make his learning personal, relevant, and respectful of his individual learning style. The New Hampshire Vision for Redesign has done impressive work on this concept of "personalized learning" that can serve as a model for our whole country. A close friend of mine, Fred Bramante, owns a chain of music stores along the East Coast and, after serving on the state board of education in New Hampshire, envisioned a different and revolutionary approach that would center on the interests of the student rather than those of the school institution.

With the help of his parents, teachers, and community, each student drafts a learning plan. For part of each day, he studies the core curriculum. But beyond that, he is encouraged to integrate his personal passions and career ambitions into credits toward his high school diploma. What has traditionally been considered extracurricular becomes a source of academic credit. A student who takes karate lessons gets gym credits. A student who plays in a rock band gets music credits. A student who interns for the local newspaper gets English credits. The opportunities are as limitless as our children's imaginations, dreams, and talents and our communities' willingness to help them. What's brilliant is that students are able to integrate what they are studying with real-world experience so that they understand that what they learn has authentic practical value. It exchanges the make-work of many schools for something vibrant. Fred's vision is catching on, and rightfully so.

Local businesses should participate to ensure that they have home-grown talent to fill their jobs. Community colleges should get involved to encourage students who were at risk of dropping out to see themselves as college material and to ensure that their transition to higher education is seamless and won't require remedial classes.

Students don't have to sit in the classroom all day, staring out the window and watching the clock. Let's take the walls and roof off our classrooms and realize that they should encompass the entire community. In fact, in the age of the Internet, they should encompass the whole world.

We are a nation proud of our respect for the individual, yet for too long our high schools have been cookie cutter, one size fits all. Let's encourage the individuality of our children; let's acknowledge that each one has his special God-given gifts, his unique contribution to make to America. One can play the violin like an angel, and another does science experiments that will help us achieve energy independence. Transforming our schools with personalized learning won't just lift our graduation rates. It will lift our children into more successful and satisfying lives.

Art and Music Education

The twenty-first century will belong to the creative; they will thrive and prosper, both as individuals and as societies. The creative ones will be the competitive ones. While you can't teach creativity the way you do state capitals and multiplication tables, you can nurture it by offering art and music to all of our students, all the way through school. I believe that the secret weapons for our remaining creative and competitive in the global economy are art and music, what I call our "weapons of mass instruction."

Studies have shown a direct correlation between music education and math scores. Music develops both sides of the brain and improves spatial reasoning and the capacity to think in the abstract. Music teaches students how to learn, and that skill is transferable to learning foreign languages, algebra, or history.

Art and music education levels the differences in academic performance among students from different socioeconomic backgrounds and reduces delinquent behavior. Art and music education results in what all parents and school districts are looking to brag about—higher SAT scores.

Some children decide early on that they're not good at school and they hate it. Art and music can save these children, can keep them in school. For them, biology may be broccoli and Spanish may be spinach, but when they get to art class or band practice, that's a hot fudge sundae. If it weren't for these opportunities, where they feel successful and worthwhile, where they're enthusiastic and engaged, many students would drop out of school. According to research by the Education Commission of the States, there is an established correlation between art and music education and high school drop out rates.

It infuriates me when people, especially my fellow conservatives, dismiss art and music as extracurricular, extraneous, and expendable. To me, they're essential to a well-rounded education.

In reality, creativity doesn't really have to be "taught" because it is naturally "caught" by every child. Do you have to beg a three-year-old to sing or a four-year-old to draw pictures or a five-year-old to playact various roles when playing fireman, doctor, or parent? What happens between the naturally creative early years and the bored-to-death teenage years? Those years are spent in a classroom in which students are told to sit down, be quiet, face forward, get your head in the book, and be still. Students today aren't dumb—the people who run the educational establishment, who want to create a conveyor belt that treats students like parts in a manufacturing plant (like the one in the Pink Floyd videos), are the dumb ones. And there's no reason to let it stay that way.

CHAPTER SEVEN

Leave Your Campsite in Better Shape
Than You Found It

We Need to Take Responsibility for the Environment

My weekly television show, *Huckabee,* on the Fox News channel, is taped in Times Square, the heart of teeming Manhattan. A walk through that district can give you a slight case of sensory overload, as you might know from experience. A cacophony of noise, pedestrians and cyclists right next to you, the glitter of huge digital jumbotrons—yes, today's "Gotham" is a long way from Hope, Arkansas, in the 1950s.

Just a quick walk from the studio to a Starbucks on the corner requires quick-witted navigation through a churning sea of humanity. And every one of these people, each of these swiftly moving pedestrians—some forging straight ahead, some blocking the sidewalk to shout into cell phones—has a unique story. It's humbling. So many millions of human beings dealing with their individual problems, hopes, failures, and triumphs.

Sometimes, though, when I'm making my way down Broadway, one story in particular pops into my mind. It's about a peculiar, frail young boy who grew up in that neighborhood in the 1860s, during the Civil War. Wearing thick glasses to correct his poor eyesight, he was nearly debilitated by recurring bouts of asthma that would render him limp, struggling to breathe.

His mother would sometimes send him up Broadway before breakfast to buy fresh strawberries at the outdoor market. One morning, he was struck by an exotic sight: a dead seal that had been caught in the harbor displayed on a slab of wood along with the mounds of fish, vegetables, and bread. This was, of course, more than a hundred years before seals were designated a protected species, but the boy had never seen this glistening marine mammal. His heart raced as it somehow brought to life the oceangoing adventure tales he loved to read. For some time, he stared at the seal in awe, until he suddenly realized he'd better get himself home in time for breakfast. I don't know whether or not he remembered to buy those strawberries.

When he returned the next day, he was excited to find the seal still there. He was on a mission, having brought a ruler in order to measure every dimension and characteristic of the animal. Passersby surely scratched their heads at the sight of this scrawny kid fastidiously recording his data in a small notebook. As it turned out, he dreamed of preserving the carcass in order to author a natural history, but he had no way of doing so. Eventually, almost all of the animal was sold off for its skin, oil, and meat, but the market keeper, well aware of the boy's intent curiosity, gave him the seal's skull.

The boy raced home with it and, before a small audience of cousins, declared it the first specimen for their new collection. On his bedroom door he hung a sign that boldly declared: ROOSEVELT MUSEUM OF NATURAL HISTORY.

True story. And if you haven't guessed by now, that peculiar, sickly (and many would later say "aggravating") little boy with the goggly specs and fertile imagination was Theodore Roosevelt, who would become the most ardent conservationist (as well as the only amateur ornithologist and zoologist) ever to occupy the White House. Hungry from such a young age for knowledge about nature, he would grow up to set aside 160 million acres as protected federal lands during his presidency, so that Americans could enjoy these preserves for centuries to come. Or as Lyndon Johnson once put it, so that we could see "a glimpse of the world as it was created, not as it looked when we got through with it."

Roosevelt was a complex, charismatic man about whom volumes have been written, and many more will follow. But the principal thing I admire about his passion for the natural world was his recognition that nature doesn't exist apart from humanity: It is part of humanity, and vice versa; we are all a part of nature. He understood that sensible existence requires a balance. Today, when we use nature's resources for our benefit, we must do so responsibly and judiciously, so that the generations that follow us can follow suit. And so forth, ad infinitum.

What I've just described is now widely discussed as "sustainability," but it's not a new concept in America and wasn't even in Roosevelt's time. The Iroquois people, for example, who have lived off American soil for centuries, devised the doctrine of "seven-generation sustainability." In other words, all decisions, environmental or otherwise, should be made in light of the impact they were likely to have on the next seven generations. For many reasons, generations have become longer than they were even early in the twentieth century, but just as a workable yardstick, let's estimate that seven generations would be about two hundred years. Now try that measure on what's happening to nature in your town or neighborhood. Probably not fitting that ideal, I'd guess.

The same idea was phrased another way by the Boy Scouts of America, as I recall from my scouting years: "Leave your campsite in as good or better shape than you found it." The rule was strictly enforced, at least in my day. I learned the important lifelong lesson that the land and its resources are for our use and enjoyment, not our abuse and destruction.

On this point, Roosevelt argued, "To waste, to destroy, our natural resources, to skin and exhaust the land instead of using it so as to increase its usefulness, will result in undermining in the days of our children the very prosperity which we ought by right to hand down to them." His conviction inspired generations of conservationists (and conservatives) to share his passion. In fact, it was Ronald Reagan who explicitly defined the connection between conservation and conservatism: "What is a conservative but one who conserves? This is what we leave to our children. And our great moral responsibility is to leave it to them either as we found it or better than we found it." For him, the lesson of the campfire applied to the whole of nature.

But both men, if you read carefully, avoided making the mistake of those fervent environmentalists who believe that nature is to be protected at the expense of humanity. I mean, let's keep it real. We human beings leave a mark on the environment. How could we not? Even in prehistoric times, when the environment was altered only in ways necessary for survival (wood fires for warmth and cooking, game killed for food, forests cleared to grow crops), however small the human footprint, however much in harmony with nature, it was nonetheless there. It was inevitable. Today, of course, there are billions more beside it. In fact, in some cases, the footprint of humanity has become a defining aspect of the land. But we should not beat ourselves up over this fact. Ours is as legitimate a role in the ecosystem as has ever existed.

Ayn Rand once wrote, in answer to especially fanatic environmentalism, "Man is treated as if he were an unnatural phenomenon." You don't have to know Genesis by heart to recall that God created us as part of the natural order, and arguably the apex of it. After all, unlike the animals of the forest or the fish of the sea, we alone possess the ability to contemplate our role in, and our impact upon, the environment.

That intelligence, that ability to reason, is why Roosevelt came to believe that we have a moral responsibility to practice sensible conservation. I see it as a moral imperative, since I believe that our abilities come from God, to lay our footprint lightly, and wisely, upon the land. We should walk with moccasins, not cleats.

The Undeniable Dangers to the Environment

I'm not going to pretend to speak with scientific authority about the possibility of global warming. When well-trained climatologists and environmental scientists don't agree on the basics, what do I know? Does global warming exist as our most urgent threat to the environment? If so, is it caused by the human race, by carbon dioxide emissions from our cars and power plants, among other things?

Can't say. But I do know that while carbon dioxide alone is not dangerous to human health, those auto and industrial emissions contain hydrocarbons that are definitely harmful to us. The answer could not be simpler. We need to reduce air pollution because it is a threat to us humans, whether or not it creates a threat to the planet. By not being effective stewards of the air we breathe, we're not just making ourselves sick; we're actually killing ourselves.

Who is crazy enough to disagree with that? According to the American Lung Association, some 60 percent of us live in areas where air pollution is a proven health danger. In its various forms, it causes asthma, bronchitis, lung disease, cancer, emphysema, heart disease, and stroke—some of which, aside from lowering quality of life, can result in premature death. Of course, pollution-caused health risks are highest for babies and children. People who live near freeways—and are thus exposed to high levels of automobile fumes—have a higher-than-normal incidence of infant mortality, heart attacks, and allergies.

The major cause of emission threats is ozone. Though not a problem in the earth's upper atmosphere, where it occurs naturally, it is a tremendous health risk at ground levels, where it creates smog. So far, the best ways to reduce this form of pollution, especially during the summer smog season, are to drive less, reduce electricity use, and not burn wood.

There are exceptions to smog danger. The cleanest air is found in places like the North Dakota towns of Fargo or Wahpeton or Lincoln, Nebraska. But things are not so good in the top ten cities polluted by ozone. Los Angeles, as you'd probably guess, is number one, followed by five other California cities plus Houston, Texas, and Charlotte, North Carolina.

The health risk second to ozone is particle pollution. In other words, soot. For the record, Bakersfield, California, suffers the worst seasonal particle pollution, while the Phoenix-Mesa-Scottsdale, Arizona, axis has the most dangerous year-round. Down the list of dangerous emissions after ozone and particle pollution are carbon monoxide, lead, nitrogen dioxide, and sulfur dioxide.

This is an ugly situation. Simply put, it is vital for us, for the sake of our national health, to cut back on pollution-causing emissions. But one word of caution: Let's not rush into things and pretend to do something useful, rather than actually address the problem sensibly. Aren't you a bit tired of the celebrity types who fly in on a fuel-hogging Gulfstream jet, then are squired in a gas-guzzling limo to a thirty-thousand-square-foot home (one of six or seven they own) in order to lecture the rest of us about using too much energy? I know I am. I only listen to envirocelebs, if you will, who walk the walk. For example, I greatly admire those like Ed Begley Jr. and Daryl Hannah, who actually practice what they preach. I'm not ready, myself, to go to the lengths they do, but consistency of conviction is admirable. Hypocrisy, though popular, is not.

This goes for government entities too, not just entertainment stars. For example, until we actually produce more of our electricity from sources other than fossil fuels, it does not measurably change the environment for some states and the federal government to force all of us to subsidize plug-in electric cars by giving tax credits for them. This is a shell game: shifting the demand for gasoline into more demand for electricity. Tax policy can't solve the pollution problem by moving it from the tailpipe to the smokestack. Now, I'm not criticizing electric cars themselves. I own one myself, a golf cart ready for street use, and find it great.

Still, we have to analyze the current situation sanely. At the moment, about 40 percent of worrisome emissions are caused by the generation of electricity. And that's not going to change overnight. In the future, we will be able to use sources like wind and solar energy to produce clean electricity; so electric cars will indeed make more sense down the road, no pun intended. Right now, about 70 percent of our states have renewable or alternative energy portfolio standards in place to encourage the generation of clean electricity. A good start. But in truth these standards are not very ambitious and will be slow to take effect: Typically, they are predicted to result in 15 percent to 20 percent of all electricity being from clean sources by 2020 or 2025.

Where does that leave us right now? One simple answer is to use "smart meters" and "smart grid" technology to reduce emissions by spreading out electric usage across the day. Because smart meters charge higher rates during peak usage times, utilities have found that they're an effective way to use the marketplace to avoid peaks and valleys of demand. I'm sure you've heard some people arguing that reducing pollution is always necessarily more expensive. Not so in this case. Smart meters are definitely a win-win, giving consumers the option of reducing their bills while helping to clean the air. For instance, Salt River Project, the largest provider of electricity to the greater Phoenix metropolitan area (where, as you'll recall, particle pollution is a year-round problem), reports that its deployment of approximately five hundred thousand smart meters has conserved 135,000 gallons of fuel. How? Those clever little gizmos helped the utility process more than 748,000 customer orders, thereby avoiding more than 1.3 million driving miles for customer-service reps. Only about one in ten American households have smart meters as I write, but the Department of Energy hopes to have them installed in about one-third of homes by 2015.

By the way, my wife and I are definitely on board with this approach to pollution problems and overuse of energy. In the house we are building in the Florida panhandle, heating and cooling will be geothermal, saving up to 80 percent of the power necessary for traditional methods. Energy efficiency will be maximized with some solar panels and hopefully a rooftop wind turbine. To quote a certain froggy, it may not be easy being green, but it sure is a good thing.

We Need to Have a Coherent Strategy

I'm not building that house as some kind of stunt or experiment. I'm putting my footprint where, maybe, Teddy Roosevelt would like it to be. I think that for a simpler America, we need to pursue all avenues of alternative energy: wind, solar, hydrogen, nuclear, geothermal, biofuels (ethanol, biodiesel), and biomass. But to do that, we need to make it possible for the private sector to make sound investments in technologies and projects by setting up a coherent, consistent statutory and regulatory framework. Partly, that means addressing a persistent problem within the environmental movement: the schizophrenia that causes different groups to work at cross-purposes.

Look what happened when the Obama administration recently approved the Cape Wind project of 130 windmill-powered turbines off Cape Cod in Massachusetts. This visionary project was supported by the governors of that state, Rhode Island, New York, New Jersey, Delaware, and Maryland, as well as the Sierra Club and Greenpeace. Immediately, rival environmental groups filed lawsuits alleging that the plan violated such statutes as the Endangered Species Act, the Migratory Bird Treaty Act, the Clean Water Act, the Rivers and Harbors Act, and the National Environmental Policy Act. Until we can find a cure for this kind of schizophrenia, we will spend more time tilting at windmills than building them. Right now, the only energy generated by this project is a lot of hot air from lawyers, and I'm afraid that's one source of renewable energy that we haven't yet learned to tap.

The Case for Nuclear Power

As I've implied already, there is no one answer to our energy problem. It's also true that, much as I share in the passion for emerging renewable technologies, we're nowhere near the point at which we'll be able to discard the old "dinosaurs," natural gas and coal. The truth is, we will need to rely upon them, at least to some extent, for decades to come. While renewable sources like solar energy, for instance, offer tremendous promise, the technology is not yet refined to the point where its costs are competitive in relation to the amount of energy generated. It's simply not ready for prime time as a utility-scale generating source, although it will be one day. Meanwhile, one "old" technology that is being looked at with new enthusiasm is nuclear power.

Of the 104 American nuclear power plants operating in thirty-one states and generating about 20 percent of our nation's electricity, not one emits greenhouse gases. Moreover, contrary to any memories you may have about Three Mile Island, these plants are very safe. The Nuclear Regulatory Commission holds nuclear reactors to higher safety and security standards than plants in any other industry. If, as the Department of Energy predicts, America will need 28 percent more electricity by 2035, I simply don't see how we can get there without better utilizing the resource of nuclear energy.

That means I strongly agree with former New Jersey governor and EPA chief Christine Todd Whitman, who has pointed out, "Expanding nuclear energy makes both environmental and business sense." That's a pretty solid combination.

Not only does nuclear energy emit no greenhouse gases or regulated air pollutants, but its costs, although high on the front end, are extremely competitive with those of other energy sources. To be specific, nuclear power is generated for about two cents per kilowatt-hour, compared to nearly three cents for coal and about five cents for natural gas. Multiply those little figures, of course, and the differences in the long run can become huge. Here's another important distinction. Unlike gas or coal, which can fluctuate dizzily in price, uranium is bought up years in advance at set prices, making fuel costs a very small percentage of operating costs. What's more, uranium is both plentiful and readily available from our allies like Canada and Australia.

Of course, as I've already suggested, the downside is that it costs more to build a nuclear plant than a coal- or gas-fired facility. Also, in the past, the federal licensing/permitting process to start a new nuclear plant was about as enjoyable as being stuck in one of the nine circles of Dante's Inferno. It made doing your taxes seem like fun. But both these challenges can be sensibly addressed. Start-up costs would come down if more plants were being built. And the Department of Energy, apparently recognizing that new nuclear plants are needed to replace our nation's aging fleet, is now working with the industry to streamline the licensing process. Already more than half of all reactors have had to have their licenses extended. If we do nothing, our nuclear capacity will be decommissioned over the coming decades because of age. Considering the increasing need, that's unacceptable. Bottom line: On a number of fronts, as I hope I've shown, new nuclear simply makes sense.

Extreme Recycling

Garbage piling up in landfills, choking the roadside, creating huge dead zones in the world's oceans . . . Talk about humanity's footprint.

But if we tackle the problem head-on, this very heavy footprint can lead us on a new path toward sustainable energy.

Back in 1985 (that would be a quarter century ago, and counting), New York City approved a plan to build plants that would be able to convert city garbage into power—kind of like a new form of Dumpster diving. Were they effective? No way to know. The plants were never built; the city currently dumps all of its waste in other states. But hope springs eternal in the City That Never Sleeps, I guess, because a former sanitation commissioner, Norman Steisel, and a former director of sanitation policy, Benjamin Miller, are now urging that those plants be built at last. According to their research, burning the city's nonrecyclable garbage in waste-to-energy plants would provide energy for almost 150,000 households, thus saving almost three million barrels of oil. There's also, ironically, a potential political plus: This would be a powerful way for New Yorkers to thumb their noses at terrorists whose plots are being supported with our payments for Middle Eastern oil.

Then there's sewage, which we create in large volume. But if treated, sewage becomes sludge, which burns very efficiently. In a 2007 report, the EPA estimated that if treatment plants nationwide converted sewage into electricity, almost 350,000 households could be powered. In terms of the total emissions that could save, it would be like having almost half a million fewer cars on the road.

Offshore Drilling

If you know me, you know that I firmly believe in a limited federal government (keep it simple) that we can depend on to do a *few* things well. Very well. As President Lincoln said, "The role of government is to do for the people what they cannot do better for themselves." Amen to that.

But now we're going to go into deep waters here, pun intended, because the horrific oil spill in the Gulf of Mexico in 2010 was a complex event that provoked complex challenges, both scientific and political. First off, let's not forget that the oil deep beneath those waters is precious and belongs to all of us. And the same goes for the fragile ecosystem of the nearby coast and offshore islands. The oil is there for us to use, but the beaches, wetlands, marshes, and estuaries, along with the plant and animal life they support, are definitely not there for us to destroy in the process. (Remember Roosevelt, the Iroquois, Reagan, and your own good sense.)

Enter the explosion of the Deepwater Horizon oil rig operated by fuel giant BP and the resulting oil spill that devastated the surrounding ecosystem. Never has there been a more telling and relevant example of what can go wrong with offshore drilling. This area in the Gulf of Mexico typically provides 40 percent of the fish in America's food supply. After the spill, fishermen could not harvest the affected fish, which imperiled the local economy, not to mention the more than four hundred wildlife species that call the Gulf home.

So does this disaster make the case that deepwater drilling should be discontinued? No, it's somewhat more complicated than that. Consider the following factors:

1. The Minerals Management Service (MMS) of the Interior Department, charged with oversight of the industry, did not mind the store. Corrupt and incompetent, it collected oil royalties while also supposedly enforcing safety and environmental regulations. Oil company workers were allowed to prepare their so-called government inspection reports in pencil, and then MMS, like a bunch of kindergarteners, traced over the "answers" in ink.

2. BP and the government both demonstrated a shocking lack of foresight. Our government did not test essential

systems like the blowout preventer that failed. BP did not have, as required in some other countries, a separate, remote-controlled shutoff switch in case that happened. Also, as is required in Canada for Arctic drilling, a relief well should have been drilled at the same time as the primary well.

3. A fire boom can burn off 75,000 gallons of oil an hour, but it took the government about a week to get a single boom to the site, much less a number great enough to perhaps contain the spill far from shore. Similarly, there weren't enough containment and absorption booms to protect the shoreline. According to Thad Allen, whom Obama put in charge of dealing with the catastrophe, the feds didn't "envision" ever having to lay boom all along the Gulf Coast at the same time. Seems to me that our government didn't envision much of anything except sunshine and lollipops.

It soon became clear to all of us, I believe, that BP was more focused on saving time and money than on saving lives and nature. Meanwhile, the response of the utterly inept Obama administration was a disaster that added to the disaster. Clearly not ready for prime time in a crisis, the president was long on photo ops and tough-sounding speechmaking but failed to take the actions that could have accelerated the saving of the Gulf Coast. Appalled by the delays and mistakes, I felt I was watching the equivalent of a major car pileup on the freeway with multiple injuries to which, instead of dispatching ambulances, fire trucks, and paramedics equipped with the "jaws of life," the authorities sent a vanload of personal-injury lawyers to pass out business cards and drum up some litigation!

Oil and Tears Don't Mix

Some of you may remember that classic TV public-service spot from the 1970s that featured a lone Indian, Iron Eyes Cody, as part of the "Keep America Beautiful" campaign. As he stands somberly beside the road, someone in a passing car callously tosses out trash that lands at his feet. The close-up on his face reveals tears in his eyes. Simple but powerful.

As other powerful images of human-caused destruction flooded the airwaves after the BP spill, especially wildlife covered in thick coats of petroleum and beaches stained by oil slicks and tar balls, I could almost picture Cody taking it all in. I could also imagine another nature lover on the scene, a man who could often be found about the White House grounds making notes on the birds inhabiting the trees there. I believe old "T.R." might shed a tear or two at the sight of a brown pelican struggling with the oil-soaked sand clumping in its feathers. After all, he used the power of the Oval Office to create fifty-one federal bird reserves, protecting many specific species, including, yes, the eastern brown pelican. I don't imagine Teddy weeping for long, though. Instead, I see him swiftly walking (softly, perhaps) to BP headquarters and pulling out that "big stick" he was known to use on occasion.

Sadly, we don't need to imagine either Iron Eyes Cody or Theodore Roosevelt shedding tears for the Gulf. Unforgettably, we saw over and over on TV news how coastal residents were shedding tears that were all too real. Crying over spilled milk, we're told, does not make sense. But a million gallons of oil a day? That's another matter entirely.

Rahm Emanuel, President Obama's former chief of staff, is fond of saying, "Never let a serious crisis go to waste." Whatever his political reasons might be for saying this, a case can be made for looking for whatever silver lining can be found in this migrating cloud of oil. Right now, that might seem wishful thinking or downright impossible. But perhaps the nation has been shocked enough by the spill, the most serious environmental disaster we've ever suffered, to reevaluate our foolish dependence of fossil fuels, heighten our environmental awareness, redefine the role we expect government to play, and become inspired to create the role we should play ourselves.

So how to proceed? First, as I suggested earlier in this chapter, we should aggressively pursue research and development of alternative sources of energy. Second, we should realistically understand that this vast, oil-dependent nation cannot be freed from the use of fossil fuels by the next election cycle. (In other words, my "green" friends, don't even bother putting that in your platform just yet.) What we can and must start doing, however, is accelerating a transition from dependence on *foreign* to dependence on *domestic* oil. As it stands now, we are virtual slaves to oil-producing nations in the Middle East whose leaders delight in becoming obscenely wealthy at our expense. This dependence, to say the least, is not necessary to our survival, since we have within our own borders far more oil reserves than the average American thinks. If we made the right choices, we could use these resources to slake our thirst for oil for generations to come. So why don't we? Well, unfortunately, much of our reserves lie beneath the sea offshore or in areas where drilling, according to many environmentalists, would be unacceptable because of possible damage to the surrounding area. That's a tough battle, but it must be resolved.

For one thing, the issue is not just about energy; our national security is also deeply involved—in ways that might not be readily apparent. Once in a while, you read something so shocking that it forces you to sit up and say, "Whoa, this is outrageous; this is insane!" That's exactly what I did when I read Thomas Friedman's *New York Times* column on July 24, 2010. He reported that retired Brigadier General Steve Anderson, once General Petraeus's senior logistician in Iraq, explained that "over 1,000 Americans have been killed in Iraq and Afghanistan hauling fuel to air-condition tents and buildings. If our military would simply insulate their structures, it would save billions of dollars and, more importantly, save lives of truck drivers and escorts." Battlefield casualties, even accidents, are inevitable in war, but I'd hate to be the father of a soldier killed under these easily preventable circumstances.

The story is even more heartbreaking when you consider that our military, while using some 130 million barrels of oil each year, is concerned about the future availability of oil supplies. Because the national-security implications are obvious, the military has made a priority of minimizing its oil dependency by researching other fuel for use in its aircraft and vehicles. To take one promising example of an alternative fuel, analysts have become interested in the potential of algae. Because it basically requires only flat land and sunlight, it should be relatively easy to produce at our bases here and overseas or even out in the field.

And while we can be horrified by the oil usage–related unnecessary deaths reported by Friedman, let's not forget about the national-security threat that we face every day because of our dependence on foreign oil. Countries, like Saudi Arabia, that make billions from us like to showcase glittering new public works projects and the like. But behind the walls they are also funding the very schools, or madrassas, that recruit, radicalize, and then train impressionable children for what is essentially the Future Terrorists of the World Club. At the same time, their so-called charities funnel money to terror cells. How can we, for even a moment, let ourselves forget this evil connection? It is expensive enough to pay for our side in the war on terror; we have to stop paying for both sides. In short, oil has not just shaped our foreign policy over the years; it has basically deformed it.

Thinking Outside the Barrel

Perhaps more benign, but no less troubling for our economy is the well-known law of supply and demand as demonstrated by the stunning growth of China in the last few years. It probably seems like a good thing to many that the communist country has been slowly opening doors in carefully limited ways to free-market capitalism. As we've been saying for hundreds of years in the West, capitalism works! But guess what? As the ancient Chinese proverb says, "Be careful what you wish for."

One consequence is that the energy demands of China's population of 1.3 billion (and counting) are becoming increasingly voracious. Add to that the similarly mounting demands of industrializing India and other developing countries. It has been projected that the global demand for energy will triple by 2050. Where on earth, in a manner of speaking, will this supply come from, and what will it cost? Will the United States have to haggle over the counter with countries that are growing powerful and wealthy and do not necessarily have our best interests at heart? This would not be pretty.

This is the simple truth: Our current economic prosperity and superpower status depend upon readily available, reasonably priced energy. It logically follows that the future belongs to countries that have adequate, reliable sources of energy under their certain control at prices that won't impoverish them.

When prices at the pump soar, people wring their hands; when they drop, most of us return merrily to our wasteful habits. What is not often discussed is that, in addition to the direct cost of oil-related products like gasoline and heating oil for the home, each price fluctuation affects indirect costs. The price of food is affected, for example, since energy is required to produce and ship most items. America has

121

become so prosperous and powerful in part because our fuel, our food, and many other necessities have historically been relatively cheap. As a result, we've been able to invest and spend our money on other things. If those days end, our standard of living will be at great risk.

Unfortunately, we now take our good fortune for granted. The richer we've become, the more wasteful. Our parents and grandparents, literally believing in "waste not, want not," compulsively turned off lights and turned down thermostats. Do you? Used to cheap commodities, our society seems to live by the creed "Why not waste? We'll never want." For the moment, our individual wallets may be able to afford our profligate ways, even during this time of recession, but our national security and hope for long-term prosperity do not have that kind of economic cushion.

After 9/11, instead of saying, "Go shopping," President Bush should have advised, "Cut your energy consumption. Conservation is patriotism." A decade later, we can and should do just that. If we make a conscious and conscientious effort, serious and substantial conservation can happen today, not years from now. Will this country necessarily have to pay more for energy as worldwide demand rises? Not if we all recognize that conservation is the one way to pay less.

Put another way, we have to decide what energy will represent for the United States in the twenty-first century: a path to our decline or to our continued dominance? Right now, there is a five-trillion-dollar market for energy worldwide. Every minute, the world produces sixty thousand barrels of oil and consuming countries spend four million dollars on that oil. At nineteen million barrels a day, we are by far the biggest consumer, importing two-thirds of that total. China is second at about nine million barrels. But we ain't seen nothing yet, in terms of either the demand for oil or the concomitant hunger for other energy sources.

But that's where opportunity lies. We can make ourselves both richer by selling new energy technology at home and abroad and more secure by creating alternatives to oil. The potential rewards are tremendous for those who can think outside the barrel. Innovation has always been an American specialty, what we have always done better than anyone else. We meet the challenges; we win the races.

And energy entrepreneurs, encouraged by the enormous market size and profit potential, do *not* need assistance and encouragement from the federal government (meaning you, the taxpayer). The feds have quite enough problems to deal with and pay for, I think. Just let the market and consumers decide what makes sense.

I agree with Stuart Butler and Kim Holmes, who addressed this subject in an article for the Heritage Foundation, "Twelve Principles to Guide U. S. Energy Policy":

> There are many guesses as to what the "new oil" might be, but no one knows for certain—least of all, the federal government. . . . The best way to secure abundant energy sources in the future is to encourage entrepreneurs to discover them, not for agencies and congressional committees to try to pick winners with directed research, regulations, mandates, and subsidies.

On the other hand, as these writers go on to explain, there may well be good reasons for the government to put in place a regulatory system "that creates the best climate for private-sector innovation." They suggest tax-free enterprise zones that would give a new company seven years of breathing room in which to develop and grow. That seems a fair trade-off to me.

The Energy Race

During the cold war, America hustled frantically into the space race after the Soviet Union stunned the world with the launch of the first-ever satellite, Sputnik, in 1957. We were caught napping; we put the pedal to the metal. And so, a little over a decade later, we won by becoming the first country to put a man on the moon. Why was it so important to outpace the Russians? Some people still don't get it, but the victory was important on two fronts: America produced amazing new technologies in order to win the contest, and we also asserted our place as the dominant force in the global economy.

Today, without quite so much fanfare and public understanding, we are engaged in a very similar race, an energy race with China. As her control over the world's resources grows exponentially, we face a simple question: In a decade, will we have won this critically important race? Will we again, in other words, produce amazing new technologies in order to win and also prove ourselves still the dominant force in the global economy? Well, here's the simple answer: No, unless we make a priority of unapologetically committing our nation to being second to no other in the creation and use of renewable, reliable, environmentally friendly, inexpensive, and domestically produced energy. I make no apologies for arguing that to do so we need to return to being unabashedly American and much less "globalist" in our national character. Cooperate with other nations of the world, when it makes sense? Of course we should cooperate, but never capitulate. Letting ourselves lose the energy race would be, undoubtedly, a form of capitulation.

I believe that's what David Pumphrey, senior fellow at the Center for Strategic and International Studies, meant when he wrote, "There is little doubt that China's growing consumption changes what ability we have to control our own destiny within global energy markets." Translation: When China becomes a huge energy customer able to pay whatever the market demands, it will jeopardize the ability of the United States to retain its position as an unchallenged superpower.

Here are some specific hints of what's likely to come. Just recently, in 2009, China outpaced us as the country that uses the most energy, 2.25 billion tons of oil equivalent (meaning the total of all sources of energy in play) versus our 2.17 billion. For the hundred years before that, the United States annually used more energy than any other country. Not surprisingly, that period coincided with our becoming the richest and most powerful country in the history of the world. This milestone is even more significant, and startling, when you consider that just a decade ago China used only half as much energy as we did.

But the entire picture is a little more complex. On a per-capita basis, we still use five times as much energy as the Chinese. But as more of them begin to demand the kinds of high-energy products that we take for granted—cars and trucks, large appliances like dishwashers and washing machines, central heating and air-conditioning in homes, workplaces, and shopping malls—the result could be a level of control over the world's resources that could grow to unimaginable heights.

Already the astonishingly speedy switch from bicycles to automobiles in China has produced another milestone: In the first six months of 2010, the American automaker General Motors sold more cars there than here at home. Even though the company has been doing business there only since 1997, China now represents 25 percent of all its sales throughout the world. Remember, the federal government spent fifty billion dollars of your money to bail GM out (and keep the assembly lines rolling). By the way, in a somewhat similar vein, the feds gave $150 million to the Koreans to make batteries for the much-heralded Volt. What's up with that? Why aren't we producing those batteries? I mean, have I missed something, and workers in the Midwest are overemployed now? This is just another example to prove that the current tax structure and rigid regulation of the development of new technologies have combined to thwart our efforts here, while the Chinese are going full throttle in their ambition to become the world's number one economy.

Back to the energy race: China is a major producer of battery technology for cars and is also forging ahead to dominate the market in all kinds of renewable energy. As we keep seeing, the upward curve of development is steep: In 1999, the country produced merely one out of every hundred solar panels manufactured worldwide, but by 2008 it was making one in three, and it now exports more panels than anyone else. On another front, in 2009 China became the world's largest producer of wind turbines, passing Denmark, Germany, Spain, and (you guessed it) the United States.

Rest assured that China's motivation in this energy revolution is economic, not environmental. It's all about producing jobs and amassing money, not about saving polar bears or rain forests. The Chinese leaders believe that this is their moment to lift their people out of poverty while also increasing their world stature both economically and militarily.

Project Independence

One possible consequence of the rise of China for America was explained in early 2010 by Keith Bradsher, chief Hong Kong correspondent for the *New York Times*: "These efforts to dominate renewable energy technologies raise the prospect that the West may someday trade its dependence on oil from the Mideast for a reliance on solar panels, wind turbines, and other gear manufactured in China." That sounds to me like a trade we definitely don't want to make. Instead, we should trade our current situation for complete energy independence.

In fact, President Richard Nixon set out the guidelines for just such a goal back in 1973. His initiative, known as Project Independence, aimed for national energy independence by 1980, or about thirty years ago. Boy, did that not happen. Back then, we imported about 20 percent of our oil; now, as I pointed out earlier, it is almost 70 percent, at a cost of one billion dollars a day. Unfortunately, the politics of "right now" blew away the principle of protecting subsequent generations. Instant Gratification 101: When the oil-producing countries eased up on prices, we eased up on the urgency.

Since Nixon, every other president, whether Democrat or Republican, has urged us toward energy independence. So why has each one, including Obama, failed so far? Former CIA director James Woolsey summed it up in one colorful sentence in the *Wall Street Journal* on April 15, 2010: "OPEC sets oil's price at a level that exploits our addiction, but it is generally not high enough for long enough that we go cold turkey." You certainly know exactly what he means. Time after time, the alarms over Middle Eastern oil have sounded in the form of price increases and supply shortages. But instead of heeding these wake-up calls, we've always rolled over and gone back to sleep.

A Natural Bridge to the Future

Aside from the other energy alternatives I've talked about here, there are exciting new possibilities in natural gas and clean coal. President Obama dismisses natural gas, as he does oil and coal, as just another fossil fuel to be shunned rather than embraced. But not all fossil fuels are the same. Natural gas releases half as much carbon as coal and is much cleaner than oil. It is also versatile, capable of being used to create electricity, fly planes, power cars and trucks, and heat our homes.

Moreover, huge quantities of natural gas have recently been uncovered in shale thanks to horizontal-drilling technologies. Consequently, the projection of American gas reserves was 60 percent higher in 2008 than in 2004, suggesting that we have enough to last almost a century. At the same time, as oil has become more expensive, gas has gone down in price.

For all of these reasons, a recent MIT study predicted that natural gas will provide from 20 percent to 40 percent of our energy over the next thirty years or so. As with every other resource, there are challenges, and we can't let the exploration companies have unrestricted free rein, since careful attention must be paid to any pollution of adjacent water supplies and other potential environmental impacts caused by the hydraulic fracturing that is used to release the gas.

But this improved technique for capturing gas has significant strategic implications, starting with bad news for the likes of Russia and Iran. Prior to the discovery of the potential of our beds of shale nationwide, those two countries were believed to control more than half of the world's natural gas. Now there won't be the expected demand for access to their supplies, meaning less wealth and power for them from this particular resource.

It's not likely that natural gas will turn out to be the "forever" solution, but it will be useful as a transition or bridge fuel. That is recognized and admitted even by those who are almost single-mindedly pushing for renewables. In other words, if we're sensible, we can use natural gas to buy us the time we need to achieve the long-term goal of making alternative energy both cheaper and more practical.

During that time, we can work to make clean coal a reality by perfecting carbon capture and storage in an economically feasible way. Nature has given us 30 percent of the world's coal, so we would be foolish to ignore the potential of this resource. While we've been leading in the race to produce clean coal, our victory is by no means assured.

Finally, we have to continue developing more effective storage systems for wind power. Who can catch the wind? America can. Because wind is intermittent, sometimes producing more power than is needed right away, it becomes unreliable when that power is wasted or not strong enough. Promising projects include creating storage batteries that adjust the flow of the power, with computers keeping the batteries half charged as the wind picks up or dies down. Also, there is research on other possible storage systems, such as those using flywheels or compressed air.

Throughout this chapter, always mindful of Teddy as that thoughtful and creative student of nature and its relationship to humankind, I've been working with the underlying theme that we Americans must do three things to preserve our freedoms: feed ourselves, fuel ourselves, and fight for ourselves (that is, we have to manufacture our own weapons of defense). Whenever we have to depend on foreign sources for any of the three, we have in effect outsourced our freedoms, because other countries might not always be friendly to us and our goals.

Never should we trade away our independence—no matter what form it comes in. Not ever.

CHAPTER EIGHT

Good Fences Make Good Neighbors

We Need Immigration Reform That Works

The notion of America as a great "melting pot" goes all the way back to at least the 1780s, when it was used to describe a young country in which various cultures and ethnicities could "melt together" into a more homogeneous whole. Somewhere along about the 1970s, proponents of multiculturalism started chafing at the idea that cultural identities might be lost in a melting pot and began favoring the "salad bowl" concept, where disparate elements mix but still remain unique. Quibbling over metaphors, perhaps, but whether you prefer the melting pot or the salad bowl vision of America, one thing is certain: Ours is a nation of immigrants. If you don't believe me, ask a Native American sometime. Most of our family trees (mine, for instance) felt the spray of saltwater at some point, as our forefathers crossed oceans to seek out a better life in a new land called America.

But the important thing to remember, whether you prefer one metaphor over another, is that in both cases we're talking about working from measured ingredients—coordinated, controlled, legal immigration, which has literally helped make America the country it is today.

And immigrants continue to make important contributions. For instance, almost half of Silicon Valley's venture capital–funded start-ups were cofounded by immigrants. If you'd seen a six-year-old Russian boy entering the United States in 1979, could you have imagined he would one day grow up to cofound Google and become one of the wealthiest men in the world, creating twenty thousand high-tech jobs in the process? No one did, but that's exactly what happened in the case of Sergey Brin. Immigrants often bring a unique perspective and are motivated to match with hard work the many opportunities America has to offer—and that in itself is the very nature of the American dream. We're all the better for it.

But most of today's illegal immigrants bear little resemblance to their predecessors from previous generations. We can no more fault a man or woman for wanting to live in the United States than we can fault our own forefathers who sought a better future here. However, when our forefathers came to America, it was to be Americans—to live here and become a part of the fabric of this great country. In too many cases, illegal border crossers have no intention or desire to spend their lives in America but are coming simply for economic gain, to make money to send back to their families in Mexico or Central America. This creates a shadow culture living "off the grid," never truly putting down roots in this country.

It's all too easy to view illegal immigration as a battle between "us and them." The toll this issue is taking on our people can be seen in the faces of those protesting both sides of the issue. The debate has become a powder keg nearing a flash point in some areas of the Southwest. Images on television of Anglos and Latinos screaming in each other's faces bear too close a resemblance to ugly scenes from the American civil rights movement for my comfort. As president, George W. Bush said something I will always remember: "We cannot build a unified country by inciting the people to anger, or playing on anyone's fears, or exploiting the issue of immigration for political gain. We must always remember that real lives will be affected by our debates and decisions, and that every human being has dignity and value, no matter what their citizenship papers say."

When they live their lives in fear of being discovered, illegals neither fully benefit from nor contribute to society. One example would be an alien afraid to report a crime for fear of being arrested himself. Or the case Tom Brokaw documented of a family of illegal aliens who, when struck by the stomach flu, bought penicillin without a prescription from a local meat market, afraid to visit a clinic or hospital. The uncle nervously guessed at an appropriate injection amount for his two-year-old niece. This is not the American dream; America is not a third-world country, but this shadow America might as well be one.

It's time to stop accepting illegal immigration as a necessary evil. One attorney who defended a large food processor in an immigration case commented, "If we didn't have immigrant labor in this country we'd all die of scurvy, because no one would pick an orange." I refuse to lean on this crutch. If we have jobs in this country that only the most desperate souls will take, for less than a living wage, that's a wage problem, not an immigration problem, and we need to deal with it as such. Other employers will tell you we've bred a generation of entitled kids who think they're "too good" to work summers digging a ditch on a construction site or washing dishes at a restaurant. Here again, that's a parenting problem, not an illegal immigration problem.

If we successfully stem the tide of illegal workers in America and then come to the conclusion that there are workforce needs we cannot fulfill domestically, then we can address those needs by upping the quota of low-skilled workers we allow to immigrate legally or by increasing the number of temporary work visas to accommodate seasonal labor or whatever the specific workforce need may be. But turning a blind eye to entire industries built on illegal immigrant labor is no answer. It may seem cheap in the picking, but that's a bushel of fruit that comes with a heavy cost in the larger scheme of things.

We need to get our own house in order and stop accepting that we can build an economy on the backs of illegal immigrants living in a shadow society. That's not an economy; it's a delusion. So let's be clear: Wanting to secure our border with Mexico isn't about xenophobia or racism or a belief that America is an exclusive club for white Anglo-Saxon Protestants or anything of the sort—it's about enforcing the law. And the law has a purpose: to make our country stronger and safer for everyone. Legal immigration makes our country stronger, while illegal immigration could prove to be our undoing.

No More Amnesty

In his major speech on immigration at American University on July 1, 2010, President Obama once again, just as he did with ObamaCare, tried to cram something down our throats that we don't want and that is wrong for our country—amnesty for illegal immigrants.

In his speech, he blamed Arizona for passing a controversial anti-illegal immigration law, and he blamed Republicans for supporting it. "Unfortunately, reform has been held hostage to political posturing and special interest wrangling," he said. No, he had it backward—securing the border has been held hostage to ideas like amnesty; it has been held hostage to political posturing.

"States like Arizona have decided to take matters into their own hands," Obama said. But why did they take matters into their own hands? The job of the federal government is to *define* and *defend* our borders. We can't be free if we aren't safe, and we aren't safe if our boundaries are ignored routinely by those without respect for our laws. Wasn't it only because the federal government threw up its hands and refused to do its job that Arizona decided to take matters into its own hands? President Obama called the Arizona law "ill conceived" when his own amnesty plans were ill conceived and contrary to the will of the people.

The American people have been burned by the failed immigration "reforms" of 1965 and 1986, which didn't seal our border and only made the problem worse. Amnesty doesn't just reward those who have broken our laws; it encourages more people to come. If we don't take our own laws seriously, why should those who want to come here? Having been duped before, the American people loudly and angrily rejected yet another amnesty bill when it was on the table in 2007—Congress got an earful and quickly backed off.

But it pushed the same poison again in 2010. Typically, when someone from Washington talks about "immigration reform," they're talking about amnesty. The "blueprint" presented by Senator Chuck Schumer of New York in April 2010 was just the same old Democrat call. He wanted illegals currently here to pay a fine and back taxes and then have a "provisional status" for eight years. Amnesty was and is always a terrible idea. Think about it—if you let it be known that there is a program whereby once you're in the country you'll be allowed to stay, what message does that send to someone contemplating an illegal border crossing? Get in at all costs! Once you're here, you'll be set. That's been the case not just in America, where the 1986 amnesty law gave us triple the number of illegals over the course of the following twenty years, but also in Europe, where amnesty programs have produced similar unintended consequences. It's just human nature—amnesty incentivizes illegal border crossing. It's a carrot, not a stick. And amnesty would be especially disastrous when millions of Americans are looking for jobs.

President Obama's immigration speech and Senator Schumer's blueprint were both consistent with the message Obama allegedly gave to Senator Jon Kyl of Arizona in a one-on-one meeting at the White House. According to Kyl, Obama told him the Democrats didn't want his administration to secure the border because then Republicans wouldn't negotiate on comprehensive immigration reform. What the president doesn't seem to understand is that securing the border is not a political bargaining chip; it is a federal obligation and duty.

Securing the border is also a national-security issue and an important part of the war on terror. There are Syrians, Sudanese, Iranians, Afghans, Iraqis, Lebanese, Nigerians, Pakistanis, Saudis, Somalis, and Yemenis being caught trying to sneak across our border with Mexico—and I don't think all these Muslims are coming to pick fruit or mow our lawns.

Arizona on the Front Lines

What's known in Arizona as Senate Bill 1070 (formally known as the Support Our Law Enforcement and Safe Neighborhoods Act) has become a lightning rod in the national debate over illegal immigration. And Governor Jan Brewer, who stepped into the job when Janet Napolitano (who had previously vetoed similar measures) left Arizona to become secretary of homeland security, is bravely holding that lightning rod despite the storm surrounding her. The fact of the matter is, Arizonans can't afford the luxury of debating illegal immigration as an esoteric policy discussion—for them, it's a matter of frontline border security. As the state with the highest incidence of illegal border crossings, Arizona has an estimated 460,000 illegal immigrants, and in the words of Governor Brewer, Arizonans "have been more than patient waiting for Washington to act. But decades of federal inaction and misguided policy have created a dangerous and unacceptable situation." Even Arizona's Democratic congresswoman Gabrielle Giffords defended the law, saying her constituents are sick and tired of the federal government failing to protect the border and calling the current situation "completely unacceptable."

Let's be clear on what Arizona's controversial law actually does—it tasks Arizona law enforcement officers with . . . well, enforcing the law. Controversial, huh? Federal law requires certain aliens to register with the federal government and carry their registration documents at all times. What the Arizona law does (at least the part that's drawing so much attention) is obligate a law enforcement officer, when making a lawful stop, detention, or arrest, to make an attempt to determine a person's immigration status if there is probable cause to suspect the person is an alien not in possession of the required legal documents. Basically, it tasks state and local law enforcement with helping enforce federal immigration law. This is Arizona trying to step in and get the job done where the feds are not. It's a strategy called "attrition through enforcement," and to me it sounds an awful lot like plain old law enforcement.

President Obama doesn't see it this way and said, "Our failure to act responsibly at the federal level will only open the door to irresponsibility by others. . . . And that includes . . . the recent efforts in Arizona." By calling Arizona irresponsible, he turned the truth on its head. Arizona was the one acting responsibly here, the one being a grown-up, by simply trying to enforce our existing immigration laws.

President Obama's criticism of Arizona contradicted his own 2010 National Drug Control Strategy, which explicitly states that our borders "must be secured," recognizing that "uncontrolled drug trafficking contributes to violence, kidnapping, robberies, and other crimes throughout the country, but *especially in border areas.*" (Emphasis added.) This was precisely what the Arizona law was designed to deal with.

Drug trafficking has made Phoenix the kidnapping capital of the United States, second in the world to Mexico City. But just as illegals wouldn't come if we didn't give them jobs, they wouldn't come if we didn't provide a market for their drugs. The 2009 National Survey of Drug Use and Health found that twenty-one million Americans (ages twelve and older) admitted using illegal drugs within the last month.

Instead of securing the border, the Obama administration put up signs in Arizona warning Americans not to travel on their own roads, in their own country, because of drug-related violence. The signs read

"DANGER—PUBLIC WARNING, TRAVEL NOT RECOMMENDED." The administration surrendered sovereignty over our territory, ceding it to lawless thugs, as if we were Somalia or Yemen.

How Dare You Enforce the Law!

Governor Brewer asked President Obama for more troops for the border, and his response was to send a busload of lawyers instead. The Arizona law finally pushed the federal government into taking action—unfortunately, it decided to sue Arizona! On July 6, 2010, the Department of Justice filed suit against Arizona in U.S. District Court asking that the Arizona law be declared unconstitutional. Immediately after it was signed by Brewer, Janet Napolitano and Attorney General Eric Holder began criticizing the law. It wasn't long before they reluctantly had to admit they'd not bothered to actually read it yet. Meanwhile, the president characterized it as "a misdirected expression of frustration over our broken immigration system." I consider his lawsuit a misdirected expression of frustration over Arizona's calling him out on that broken system. The lawsuit wastes taxpayer money and government resources that should be used to go after illegals, not the American victims of government abdication.

The Arizona law is constitutional because it is consistent with federal law, and the state was simply conducting "concurrent enforcement." A state law does not violate the Constitution's supremacy clause unless it conflicts with federal law. For instance, if Arizona were to declare that anyone crossing the border could become a citizen in a month, such a law would violate the supremacy clause because it would contradict federal law. Holding illegals accountable to the law is, by its very nature, simpatico with the law.

As a former governor, I can imagine how furious Governor Brewer was to hear about the lawsuit from an interview Secretary of State Hillary Clinton gave in Ecuador, rather than from the courtesy of a phone call from the Justice Department. Justice rejected the State Department's request that it announce the lawsuit before Secretary Clinton's Latin America trip.

In one of the most outrageous—and bizarre—episodes in all of America's diplomatic history, Assistant Secretary of State Michael Posner, during a sit-down with the Chinese about human rights in May 2010, spoke unabashedly about the Arizona law as if it were somehow analogous to China's horrific record of evil toward its own citizens—as if asking someone for identification, when the police have stopped him for a valid reason, is like mowing down an unarmed civilian with a tank or forcing a woman pregnant with her second child to have an abortion. It seemed like a *Saturday Night Live* or *Daily Show* satire, but Posner was serious. It made me wonder if Posner isn't an alien himself—an alien from another planet!

Perhaps the most telling statement, you might even call it a Freudian slip, in this whole ordeal came from the office of Mexican president Felipe Calderón: "The Mexican government condemns the approval of the law" and "the *criminalization of migration*, far from contributing to collaboration between Mexico and the state of Arizona, represents an obstacle to solving the shared problems of the border region." (Emphasis added.) President Calderón makes an interesting choice of words here—it's not "migration" that Arizona has criminalized; it's *illegal* migration (which was criminalized by the federal government) that Arizona is seeking to curb by simply enforcing the law. This is a distinction Calderón and many others seem unable to comprehend.

Arizona is not the only state that is fed up. In the first quarter of 2010, almost 1,200 bills and resolutions dealing with immigration were proposed in forty-five states. In fact, a recent *New York Times/CBS News* poll showed that 89 percent of Americans believe either that our immigration system needs some "fundamental changes" or that it should be completely rebuilt. But states shouldn't have to do this. It is one of the few things the national government is actually supposed to do, and yet, despite how big the government has gotten and how much they spend, the feds can't seem to take responsibility. Instead of policing the states, they should police those who are actually breaking the law.

Secure the Borders

In 2006, Congress voted to build a fence along our border with Mexico, and even though President George W. Bush began work on it before he left office, President Obama halted that work in 2010. We must finish the fence. With apologies to Kevin Costner, if we build it, they *won't* come.

In May 2010, President Obama agreed to send up to 1,200 National Guard forces for a year to support our border patrol. This was nowhere near enough, and their mission should not have been limited to a year. Under President Bush's "Operation Jump Start," we had six thousand National Guard at the border, which is what Governor Brewer asked President Obama for.

But securing our border is a broader concept than simply preventing people from crossing. It includes discouraging people from approaching the border in the first place. Illegals must view our border not as an obstacle to overcome but as a dead end with no opportunity for them on the other side. So securing our border means securing our workplaces. Illegals are doing many of our jobs only because the federal government isn't doing its job.

If illegals can't find work, those who are here will leave, and those who would consider coming will stay home. We must enforce the law, and we must go after employers with hefty fines and prison time for repeat offenders. As one attorney who represents illegal immigrants said, "It's like our border has two signs: 'Keep Out' and 'Help Wanted.'" We can't have it both ways.

In November 2009, President Obama rescinded President George H. W. Bush's "No Match" rule, under which the Department of Homeland Security tracked false Social Security numbers to find illegals and then required employers to dismiss them.

In 2008, under President George W. Bush, workplace arrests totaled about 6,000 in FY 2008. But under President Obama, these arrests fell to just 900 in FY 2010.

President Bush replaced "catch and release" with "detention and removal" after workplace raids. But President Obama has brought back "catch and release," after which illegals just disappear. He has been conducting payroll audits instead of raids. That means illegals sometimes lose their jobs, but they don't get deported; they just find other jobs.

Even when we try to bring illegals to justice, we are hopelessly ineffective. About 60 percent of illegals who are not held in jail don't show up for their hearing. About 90 percent of illegals who lose in court don't appeal the decision—why bother when it's so easy to just leave the area and move somewhere else in this country?

Americans Need Jobs Too

The Center for Immigration Studies has estimated that 1.2 million illegal Mexican immigrants went home between 2006 and 2009, more than double the number who went home between 2002 and 2005.

The Pew Hispanic Center estimated that illegal Mexican immigration in 2008–9 was one-fourth that in 2004–5.

The number of border apprehensions, which is used to determine how many people are trying to come into the country illegally, was down 23 percent in 2008–9 compared to 2007–8.

But as the economy improves, they'll try to come back. That's why we can't wait to secure the border.

The Kauffman Foundation, which studies entrepreneurial activity, found that in the last decade, immigrants started one-quarter of all new American high-tech companies. We should allow more foreign students receiving science degrees to stay here. As I said at the outset, the problem isn't immigrants; it's immigrants that we don't choose. This is our country; we have to decide who comes here and who stays here.

We need fewer people looking for low-skilled work and more people who not only can perform high-skilled work themselves but also will create high-skilled jobs for Americans. This is a notion that goes back to early America, when George Washington wrote in a 1794 letter to John Adams that there was no particular need to encourage immigration, "except of useful mechanics and some particular descriptions of men or professions."

California is a perfect example of what happens when we are overrun by uneducated, unskilled people who are a burden rather than an asset. In 1970, California had the seventh-most-educated workforce in this country. By 2008, with its immigrant population having tripled, California was dead last, and large numbers of U.S.-born Hispanic students remain "English language learners" through most of their school years due to insufficient academic and language skills.

The Federation for American Immigration Reform (FAIR) issued a report in July 2010 entitled "The Fiscal Burden of Illegal Immigration on United States Taxpayers," which found that illegal immigration costs all of us $113 billion a year, with $84.2 billion coming from state and local governments and $28.6 billion from the federal government. The largest cost is $52 billion for education. Among our states, the largest shares were borne by California at $21.8 billion, New York at $9.5 billion, and Texas at $8.9 billion. The average American household pays $1,117 per year toward the cost of illegal aliens in our country.

If You're Stuck in a Hole, the First Thing to Do Is to Stop Digging

Immigration reform is not easy and will require a multipronged strategy. As a matter of public policy, it's like the Gordian knot—you can't untie it, and if you cut through it in one reckless stroke, you're going to have a lot of loose ends on your hands. An estimated eleven to thirteen million illegal aliens are already living among us. But we can't even begin to untie this knotty mess until we secure the border and stop the constant flow of illegal crossings adding to the problem. When you can't control entry, you don't have an immigration system; you have a free-for-all.

There is no single, clear answer to the illegal immigration problem, but there is a single, clear first step—secure the border. Only then can true immigration reform take place.

CHAPTER NINE

Bullies on the Playground Understand Only One Thing

We Need a Strong Approach to Terrorism

We all remember exactly where we were on September 11, 2001. For most of us, that day was spent glued to the TV with family or maybe coworkers as unspeakable horror unfolded. But I remember just as clearly where I was on September 11, 2002.

On that fall morning, I stood on the steps of the Arkansas State Capitol to address a group of citizens gathered to mark the one-year anniversary of 9/11 and honor those lost at the World Trade Center, at the Pentagon, and in a nondescript field in rural Pennsylvania. More than anything I said that morning, I remember the looks on the faces of those who attended, for they were neither partisan politicos nor folks with an agenda—the usual crowd in the halls of state government. Instead, they were simply Americans who had come together to share in a moment of remembrance and find strength in unity.

But I also remember how their faces changed as I told them about a guy named Richard Cyril Rescorla, better known as "Rick," who died in the World Trade Center. If ever a man was destined to leave this earth a hero, it was Rick Rescorla. He had served in the British military

145

A Simple Government

before immigrating to America and joining the U.S. Army to serve in Vietnam. He fought with distinction at Ia Drang, a famously bloody battle that was chronicled in the book and film *We Were Soldiers Once . . . and Young*. But Rick did not leave his devotion to duty on a foreign battlefield.

As chief of security for Morgan Stanley's offices in the World Trade Center, he spent much of his time assessing the risk terrorists might pose to those under his watch. As early as 1992, he warned authorities that the supporting pillars in the center's basement parking garage presented a prime target for attack. A year later, you'll recall, his warning proved all too prophetic.

Over the next decade, Rick's evacuation plans became the stuff of legend at Morgan Stanley. He insisted that everyone, from the stuffed-shirt executives to the messengers in bike shorts, learn and practice evacuation procedures on a regular basis. As a veteran of armed conflict he understood that a plan could be effectively executed in the confusion of battle only if it had been practiced in peace and reinforced until it became almost a matter of muscle memory. But more important, he understood the essential fact: The terrorists who failed in 1993 would try again.

So Rick Rescorla was prepared when the first plane struck on 9/11. While the rest of us watched without fully understanding at first and authorities urged everyone to remain calm and stay put, he ignored the ill-advised warnings and, according to plan, briskly led more than two thousand Morgan Stanley employees on twenty floors of Tower 2 down the stairs and out of the building to safety. He also made sure that the one thousand Morgan Stanley employees in nearby Building 5 were evacuated. Throughout the operation, Rick sang songs over his bullhorn, including "God Bless America," the hymn of his adopted country.

Once on the street, mission completed, most men would have called it a day. But Rick Rescorla was not like most men. He couldn't abide the possibility that someone—one of his flock—was overlooked and still inside. After seeing that his charges on the street stayed together and moved safely away from the tower, he headed back in to climb the stairs and check for stragglers. He was never again seen alive.

I told this story because it had moved me when I first heard it; it moves me to this day. It moved the crowd in Little Rock. But I could see on their faces a shift from a mood of mourning to something more. I said that the flames of the World Trade Center—the very flames that killed Rick Rescorla and so many others—achieved more than the terrorists could ever have anticipated. Those very flames, I went on, caused our great American melting pot to boil over. Whenever those waters have boiled over, throughout our history, they have snuffed out the flames of tyranny, hatred, and evil, even when they seemed to burn unchecked. At this point in my talk, I could see in the faces before me an obvious strength and resolve that reminded me that it is not in the DNA of Americans to live our lives as victims. We never have, and I pray that we never will. In fact, at the time I was addressing those folks in 2002, our nation was already mobilizing, ready to take the fight to the terrorists where they live.

Right now, I don't feel as hopeful as I did that day. I have to ask myself this question: If Rick Rescorla were here today, how could I explain to him how and why we've dropped the ball in the global war on terror? How would I explain to this hero—a man who not only saw imminent danger on the horizon but also devised and executed a simple yet effective survival strategy—that afterward, even with all the resources our nation can bring to bear, we have not followed suit?

PC Is Not a Strategy

Are we even marginally still engaged in a war on terror? In many ways, it ended when President Obama took office. Was there some final victory that I somehow didn't hear about? No, he just changed the name of our efforts to "overseas contingency operations," which doesn't make sense as English, let alone as military strategy. If the man had been in the White House on June 6, 1944, we might now know D-Day as "A Day at the Beach."

So this is the politically correct order of the day. We're not supposed to talk about "terror," for one thing, and we should especially refrain from mentioning that it is radical Islamists who are coming after us. On November 10, 2009, the president spoke at the Fort Hood memorial service to honor the thirteen soldiers (and the unborn child of one of them) who had been murdered by Major Nidal Hasan as an act of jihad. Astonishingly, as if completely ignoring the motivation behind this tragedy, he never used such words as *Islam* or *Islamist* or *Muslim*. Does ignoring the gorilla in the room mean that he's really not there?

A few months later, in May 2010, Texas congressman Lamar Smith tried to get Attorney General Eric Holder to admit that a belief in radical Islam was behind Hasan's attack, as well as Umar Farouk Abdulmutallab's failed attempt to explode a bomb in his "Under-roos" on a plane to Detroit the Christmas before and Faisal Shahzad's fizzled bomb during rush hour in Times Square earlier that month. Here is an excerpt from the congressional hearing:

CONGRESSMAN SMITH: Are you uncomfortable attributing any of their actions to radical Islam? It sounds like it.
ATTORNEY GENERAL HOLDER: I don't want to say anything negative about the religion. . . .
SMITH: I'm not talking about religion. I'm talking about radical Islam. I'm not talking about the general religion. . . .
HOLDER: I certainly think that it's possible that people who espouse a radical version of Islam have had an ability to have an impact on people like Mr. Shahzad.

This was not just a disagreement about semantics. The guys they're talking about weren't trying to blow things up (themselves included) because they were pyromaniacs; they were engaged in their own personal acts of jihad. We can only thank the Lord that they were so inept, because we were failed by the system we trusted to catch them before they could act on their hatred. If they'd had the skills to match that hatred, we would have suffered scores of casualties.

The current bizarre taboo against identifying our enemy by name reminds me of our deference to the Islamic prohibition against depicting Mohammad. We're so afraid of offending the people who are hell-bent on wiping us out that we are now playing by their rules. The naming taboo also goes to the heart of our ability to prosecute this war, a war that Osama bin Laden declared on us in 1996 and 1998, before his attacks (or overseas contingency operations) on our embassies in Tanzania and Kenya in 1998, on the USS *Cole* in 2000, and on the World Trade Center and Pentagon in 2001.

As the frustrated and incredulous Congressman Smith remarked to Attorney General Holder, "I don't know why the administration has such difficulty acknowledging the obvious. . . . If you can't name the enemy, then you're going to have a hard time trying to respond to them." Exactly! This example of PC (like so many) isn't just silly; it's downright dangerous, and also reminiscent of our failure to recognize the seriousness of the Islamic terror threat after the first attack on the World Trade Center in 1993. Rick Rescorla, though he was nowhere near the halls of national power or the inner sanctum of the intelligence community, clearly saw the writing on the wall. He correctly inferred that this failed attack was in fact a first strike in a larger offensive. How could so many others not see that?

The Roots of Terrorism

Perhaps President Obama and his administration are so wary of naming the enemy because they are fundamentally unable to distinguish between the ancient religion of Islam and the radical Islam of our day—a totalitarian ideology like its predecessors in the twentieth century, communism and fascism. While traditional Islam is not my particular cup of religious tea, I can accept it generally as a historical set of beliefs that brings purpose and unity to millions of peaceful worshipers around the globe. It is clear that most followers of Islam are as revolted by terror as we are (and, in some cases, as likely to be attacked and killed).

But radical Islam is an altogether different thing: It isn't as much a religion as it is a psychosis. Don't get me wrong: All religions must be vigilant against radical perversion, as Christians learned, for instance, from the medieval and Spanish inquisitions or the Salem witch trials. But to confuse the radical with the righteous in any religion, or to lump them together, is a tragic mistake. In the Obama administration's fear of naming the obvious, it is a tactical error.

To fight them, you have to know precisely how they think. The terrorists who scheme against us follow the ideology of the Egyptian Sayyid Qutb, the Karl Marx of Islamic extremism. His writings, which are the intellectual foundation of the movement, include the following tenet: "A Muslim has no nationality except his belief." If that's the case, the radical Islamist can have no loyalty to the United States or any other country. He is loyal only to the jihad that plots to establish an Islamist theocracy, or religion-run government, that will eventually rule a worldwide caliphate. This is a breathtaking ambition, but Qutb and his followers mean it. Political divisions are irrelevant, because lines on a map can be wiped forever away with a blood-soaked rag. This is the root explanation of why the war on terror is infinitely more complex than any prior war, in which opposing nations typically fought each other on battlefields. Terror, by contrast, happens at home. In almost any nation. Anywhere.

Although Qutb was executed by President Nasser in 1966, he and his ideas have remained alive to haunt us through his followers. He has inspired terrorists from bin Laden to the radical American-born imam Anwar al-Awlaki, now in hiding in Yemen. Al-Awlaki, in turn, inspired Hasan, Abdulmutallab, and Shahzad. He has argued that "jihad against America is binding upon myself, just as it is binding on every other able Muslim." That's a pretty clear renunciation of any claim to his citizenship, I'd think. Yet when he was added to the CIA's list of terrorists being targeted by our drones, the *New York Times* denounced this move as a planned execution by the United States of "one of its own citizens far from a combat zone." I guess they just don't get it: Yemen is a combat zone. It is, in fact, the headquarters of Al Qaeda in the Arabian Peninsula (AQAP). During the Civil War Abraham Lincoln asked, "Must I shoot a simple-minded deserter, while I must not touch a hair of a wily agitator who induces him to desert?" In any event, the CIA has reason to believe that al-Awlaki has gone well beyond being a wily agitator who preaches that attacking America is a "religious duty." Evidently, he is now actively engaged in plotting with AQAP.

Sadly, while we've become used to packing our Ziploc bags with miniature bottles of shampoo and taking off our shoes at airport security gates, some of us still have not intellectually grasped whom and what we are fighting. Unfortunately, President George W. Bush was only half right when he said that we have to fight them there so that we won't have to fight them here. In a war without borders, the truth is that we have to fight them here, there, and everywhere, even if walking sock-footed through airports and having our belongings rustled about by TSA workers does less to deter terrorism than to inconvenience travelers.

It has not helped the war that, after 9/11, too many senators and congressmen shamefully saw homeland-security funds as a great source of local pork rather than as limited, precious resources to be allocated based purely on risk. It also hasn't helped that too many in the administration are like the sputtering attorney general or Secretary of Homeland Security Janet Napolitano, who has referred to the war on terror as a series of "man-made disasters."

Politicians and pundits alike are fond of repeating that 9/11 "changed everything." It has certainly changed some things, but it hasn't changed enough of them so that we can effectively fight our enemies.

The Wrong Paradigms

For one thing, we have continued to try to fit the round peg of Islamic terrorism into the square hole of our traditional criminal justice system. Remember, we didn't choose this particular enemy or this new mode of warfare, but we must adjust our response to the circumstances. Nothing in the Constitution prevents us from defending ourselves and our country. Or, as Supreme Court justice Robert Jackson once put it, "If the court does not temper its doctrinaire logic with a little practical wisdom, it will convert the constitutional Bill of Rights into a suicide pact."

That's close to what Attorney General Holder is doing by pursuing a way to expand the public-safety exception under the *Miranda* decision, which requires that criminal suspects be read their rights. He is not only wasting his time but also jeopardizing our safety. We don't need an improved public-safety exception because, in the war against terrorists, we don't need *Miranda* at all. He also wants to delay the initial hearing for a captured terrorist suspect.

These ideas are completely wrongheaded. The criminal justice system that the Obama administration is tinkering with was designed to keep the peace, not prosecute a war. It's like zoo officials planning an extreme home makeover on the aviary to make room for the new elephant. We can't successfully wage this war if we use the wrong paradigm. *Miranda* was intended to yield admissible evidence that would be upheld in order to gain convictions. What's the connection here? What we need is usable intelligence that will keep us safe from these whack-jobs who leap up from their prayer rugs with a renewed zeal to sever our heads.

If someone steals a watch from a store in Times Square, he's a criminal who is entitled by law to *Miranda* warnings whether he's a Christian, a Muslim, or an atheist. But when a radical Islamist tries to detonate a bomb in Times Square, he's an unlawful enemy combatant. *Miranda* is irrelevant because he's attacking the country as part of a war, not because he's a Muslim. When our soldiers pulled Saddam Hussein out of the hidey-hole he'd fashioned near Tikrit in 2003, the message they delivered was not "You have the right to remain silent." Be it in Tikrit or Topeka, a terrorist is not a criminal; he is an enemy. We should be consistent in treating him as such.

Holder's efforts are only part of the ongoing legal confusion. There is conflict among lawyers at the State Department, Justice Department, and Pentagon over the limits of executive counterterrorism powers. The administration wants to rely more heavily on the Geneva Conventions, but those agreements never envisioned this type of warfare. Another dangerously wrong paradigm! The war on terror is challenging enough without our tying one hand (or both) behind our backs.

Yet another ill-advised paradigm is the use of the Foreign Intelligence Surveillance Act (FISA) to control how we monitor terrorist communications. FISA was passed in 1978 in response to possibly

A Simple Government

questionable government surveillance of members of the civil rights and anti–Vietnam War movements. But the pendulum swings. Today, New York City police commissioner Ray Kelly has properly called FISA "an unnecessarily protracted, risk-averse process." That means we are erring on the side of overprotecting e-mails and cell-phone calls while putting our lives in danger. Either FISA must be rewritten to address the current situation or a separate set of rules should govern our conduct of the war on terror.

When Will We Stop Underestimating the Enemy?

Even though Major Hasan's damning e-mail correspondence with jihadist Anwar al-Awlaki was in hand, for some reason the Joint Terrorism Task Force and the army decided to not even bother to investigate him. Their negligence let him go on to murder thirteen and wound thirty-one of his fellow soldiers, including an innocent unborn child. What were our officials thinking?

Here's another unbelievable anecdote: Before Abdulmutallab's underwear bomb at Christmas 2009, our officials thought Al Qaeda in the Arabian Peninsula didn't have the ability to attack us in the homeland. We did know that they wanted revenge for our attacks in Yemen, but we assumed that they could mount only regional responses. As John Brennan, President Obama's counterterrorism czar, would admit later, "We didn't know they had progressed to the point of actually launching individuals here."

But why didn't we know? Isn't that precisely why we've spent tens of billions since 9/11 and established the Office of the Director of National Intelligence, the Department of Homeland Security, and the National Counterterrorism Center (NCTC)? The aim was to figure out not just the aspirations of terrorists but also their capabilities. Obviously, we're not going to go on high alert for something we're convinced they can't do. You'll recall that Rick Rescorla was proved right within a year of his warning about those garage support pillars.

How many failed attempts by inept jihadists will it take to make us realize that the enemy is already here?

That's at least one lesson of Faisal Shahzad's Times Square bomb attempt in the spring of 2010. That time we were blindsided by the Pakistani Taliban, who wanted payback for our killing of their leader Baitullah Mehsud in the summer of 2009. As with the underwear bomber, we didn't see that one coming. Same excuse, believe it or not: Officials explained haplessly that they hadn't believed the Pakistanis had the ability to attack us at home.

Abdulmutallab's ineptitude in trying to ignite his underwear bomb or Shahzad's dumb move of locking his getaway car's keys in the vehicle he meant to explode might remind us of Karl Marx's warning: History repeats itself first as tragedy, then as farce. Comparing the 9/11 tragedy with the two recent farces could be misleading, though. We view these terrorists as "the gang that couldn't shoot straight" at our own peril. Any laughter is not real mirth, since we should remember that at any time, perhaps on another clear blue September morning, the line between farce and tragedy could be revealed to be as thin as a skillfully placed detonator cord. Not all of these radical zombies will be as stupid and inept as the "fruit of the loon" bomber or the "propane tankmeister."

Even when terrorists fail so miserably, we have to take them seriously—gravely seriously. They're like cockroaches. For every one we see, we should assume that there are many more lurking in the darkest corners. We have to race forward—against time, partisan sniping, bureaucratic infighting, and political correctness—to get to them before they get to us, and before they once again get it right.

The Warning Signs Are There

The story isn't over yet, and unfortunately, the more you dig, the worse it gets.

Prior to Umar Farouk Abdulmutallab's attempt to blow up that flight to Detroit, we had been given specific intelligence that Al Qaeda was planning an attack using a Nigerian. To be fair, there are lots of Nigerians, so that's not much help. But wait. Abdulmutallab's father appeared at our Nigerian embassy to report that his son had become a religious extremist and had moved to Yemen. Hello! I don't have formal training in threat assessment, and you might not either, but I think we can agree that when a guy's own father fears that he's a threat, we should consider him a threat. Nor was his son just any old Nigerian: He had a visa that allowed him to enter the United States. Do you see a problem here? These are neon-bright dots just begging to be connected. They weren't.

Just a few months later, Faisal Shahzad's capture as he tried to flee the country after his Times Square fiasco further illustrated the need to build as much redundancy as possible into the system. A Customs and Border Protection center in Virginia double-checked Shahzad's name on the final passenger list for his intended getaway flight, but he did not yet appear on the no-fly list of Emirates Airline. It seems that whenever there is a close call like this, we discover things that don't make sense—like airlines being given twenty-four hours, an absurdly long time, to check flight-list updates. The rule was immediately changed to two hours, but when a high-priority name is added, the window should be no more than fifteen or twenty minutes. It was also inexcusable, and I was amazed to see reported, that the government, so long after 9/11, had not yet assumed responsibility for checking the no-fly lists kept by airlines. When Shahzad was arrested, this takeover was still in its test phase for domestic airlines and hadn't even begun for international airlines.

We nabbed Shahzad only because of a phone number he had given customs officials when he returned from Pakistan in February 2010. Because the number was put in a database, he was pulled aside under a government policy—instituted in response to Abdulmutallab's failed bombing attempt the previous Christmas—requiring stepped-up screenings for all passengers from fourteen countries, including Pakistan. Amazingly, that program was quickly canceled. Would Shahzad have been questioned anyway, or was he caught only because of that policy? I don't know, but it seems to me that that short-lived program should have been a keeper. It was pure luck that Shahzad returned from the Middle East not long after the Abdulmutallab event. Eventually, luck runs out.

A *New York Times* profile of Shahzad contained a tantalizing nugget: A man who bought a condo from the Times Square bomber in Norwalk, Connecticut, back in May 2004 reported that the FBI's Joint Terrorism Task Force interviewed him soon afterward about Shahzad. What exactly did the government know about him six years before his failed attack? More specifically, why was he on their radar screen in the first place, and why was he then (apparently) taken off it? How in the world was he allowed to slip through the cracks, very nearly at the expense of innocent lives?

Is this just an extremely rare occurrence? Hardly. On May 18, 2010, just two weeks after the Times Square attempt, the unclassified summary of a report by the Senate Select Committee on Intelligence revealed fourteen points of failure related specifically to Abdulmutallab's attempted Christmas bombing. They included "human errors, technical problems, systemic obstacles, analytical misjudgments, and competing priorities." I find this a sad and sobering assessment of how much our government had still not fixed more than eight years after 9/11.

The committee spread the blame around. It faulted the State Department for not revoking Abdulmutallab's visa and the FBI for not being able to access the reports about him. It found that the CIA, the NCTC, and the National Security Agency were responsible for various failures in collecting, distributing, and analyzing information. To take just one example, both the CIA and the NCTC ignored our Nigerian embassy's recommendation to put Abdulmutallab on the no-fly list. Meanwhile, the former Cat Stevens, now known as Yusuf Islam, was driving wherever he went, having been deported from the United States after being caught on the no-fly list. And sweet little Alyssa Thomas, a six-year-old girl from Westlake, Ohio, remains on the list for reasons unknown, despite her parents' repeated appeals of that status. Curiouser and curiouser.

In conclusion, the committee report noted that the entire intelligence community had so narrowly focused on the threat Arabian Al-Qaeda posed to U.S. interests in Yemen that it had virtually ignored the potential for an attack on the homeland from there.

Two days after the unclassified summary was released, director of national intelligence (DNI) Dennis Blair resigned. Three strikes—Hasan, Abdulmutallab, Shahzad—and he was out. At least that's one step in the right direction.

Turf Battles

News analysis of Blair's resignation highlighted a serious security problem. Just as there were crippling conflicts between the FBI and the CIA before 9/11, turf battles among many intelligence agencies are ongoing. This remains true even though Blair's DNI position was established in 2004 specifically to head up and unify all sixteen agencies, including the CIA. In the beginning, Blair asserted the right to choose the top intelligence official in each of our embassies overseas, a decision traditionally made by the CIA station chief at each posting. When CIA director Leon Panetta objected, the White House sided with him against the newly appointed DNI. You can bet the heads of other agencies read a message there, a message that said that the White House would be calling the shots.

Meanwhile, the creation of several new bureaucracies has in no way cleared up exactly who is responsible for what. (Does anyone really expect bureaucracies to clear up rather than obfuscate?) The NCTC, also established in 2004, was intended to coordinate intelligence, mostly from overseas. Now it is seeking Obama's nod for increased authority to do analysis domestically, thus putting it on FBI turf. At the same time, officials at the Department of Homeland Security (DHS) seek greater authority to train local law enforcement and citizens to spot indications of potential violent extremism. Such an emphasis on a more local, decentralized approach could conflict with the NCTC's national effort.

Yet another approach has been suggested by Michael Sheehan, former counterterrorism chief for the State Department and the New York Police Department (NYPD). He would take the basic idea of the DHS plan but make it more structured, powerful, and independent. Essentially, he wants other cities to do what the NYPD has done: set up its own intelligence and counterterrorism units that use informants and undercover officers, much as other units fight drugs and organized crime. The NYPD is flexible enough to work with the FBI on occasion but often works on its own.

I say, since we need as many working channels as possible, let's work both top down and ground up. There's a potential for stepping on one another's toes, maybe, but I'd rather have the good guys bumping into each other than missing leads because everyone was more focused on protecting their own turf. Washington officials might be in the best position to connect the dots coming from all over the world, while locals can concentrate on providing as many dots as possible. It's better to have different perspectives and skill sets with overlapping jurisdictions than dangerous gaps in our coverage—better to have plots uncovered by several means than by none.

We Must Look in Other Directions

In addition to the threat of terrorists shooting us or blowing us up, like the three radical extremists we've been discussing, the true stuff of nightmares is that all sorts of other scenarios for attacks on our homeland abound. For example, as former CIA officer Charles Faddis has written, there is a real threat to our nuclear power plants. He cites the example of Sharif Mobley of New Jersey, who worked at five plants before allegedly joining Al Qaeda in Yemen. Since he was a maintenance worker, you might think he doesn't have information that would help terrorists mount a successful attack. You would be very wrong.

As Faddis explains, to destroy a plant you don't need access to its core, just to its cooling system, in which most components are unprotected. If a cooling system is disabled, heat will rise and melt the reactor, causing a partial meltdown of the plant. Think *The China Syndrome*. Since the security at all of our nuclear power plants is pretty much the same, Faddis warns, we now have to change the protocol at all of them, not just those where Mobley worked.

Another threat—the risk of cyberattacks that could turn our own technology against us—has been outlined by Richard Clarke, counterterrorism czar to Presidents Clinton and Bush 43. While noting that both the Pentagon's Cyber Command and the DHS are taking strong steps to defend the government against such attacks, he warns that they are not doing enough to protect our civilian infrastructure. He also believes that the Pentagon has focused too much on its offensive war capacity to the detriment of its defensive capabilities.

Clarke predicts that America would fare far worse than Russia or China in a cyberwar. Apocalyptically, he imagines that our banking system, power grids, and air and rail systems could be completely shut down, while our oil pipelines and chemical plants could be destroyed in explosions. All it would take to inflict absolute chaos on our lives and economy, in this scenario, would be some clever computer hacking. (I'm a believer: If I ever lost the use of just my ever-reliable Mac-Book, my life would certainly be chaos!)

Since we are a vast, rich, technologically advanced society, there are many other avenues of attack here for creative terrorists; we have a lot to defend on many levels. To date, for example, we haven't done nearly enough to guard against chemical and biological attacks, to protect our drinking water, or to secure our ports. Every school, shopping mall, sports stadium, place of worship, and means of public transportation offers a potential target.

The War Abroad

But the threats to the homeland, even as we remain on alert, will not go away unless we eradicate them at their source. We cannot give up on the wars in the Middle East until we've definitively finished the job there.

In Afghanistan, we seem to be darned if we do, darned if we don't. Some Afghans support the Taliban against us because they believe the propaganda that the United States wants to occupy their country long term. Ironically, others fear just the opposite: that we'll leave, allowing the Taliban to return to power. For them, working against us means eventually being on the winning side. That's kind of like paying "protection money" to the Mafia in the neighborhood; you don't want to, but not doing so would wind up being most costly.

Then there's the complicating factor of Obama's announced timetable. In Iraq, it made sense to set a timetable because it forced the Iraqi government to pull itself together and function, knowing we were going to leave it to its own devices. But that tactic can't work in Afghanistan, because there isn't enough of a central government to prod. Nor is there the infrastructure and educated middle class that exist in Iraq. Many of our troops in Afghanistan write home that life around them is so primitive they feel as if they're back in biblical times. In 2005, when I visited both countries, I was shocked by the obvious contrast. Despite the scars of war, Iraq clearly has all the ingredients in place for becoming a successful economy and nation. Afghanistan, on the other hand, reminded me of photos from the surface of the moon! In terms of the overall culture as I experienced it, I was thinking *Flintstones*.

Our success in Iraq was propelled by the troop surge, but an important factor was that the population turned against Al Qaeda, which they saw as a brutal, foreign force beholden to an extremist ideology. In much of Afghanistan, however, the Taliban is local and less feared and resented.

The tactic of a troop surge cannot be as effective in Afghanistan as in Iraq because, when we make military progress against the Taliban, President Karzai does not, or cannot, find competent officials to take hold of the cleared territory. Nor do we get a comparable "surge" in the number of honest, well-trained civil servants and police. So we're left with two kinds of failure: Our military successes create a vacuum of authority that is either quickly filled by the returning Taliban or taken over by warlords or illegitimate officials whom the Afghans see as corrupt in the vein of Tony Soprano.

Kandahar Province is theoretically run by Karzai's thuggish brother as a representative of the central government, but the Taliban is very powerful there. In a survey taken there in April 2010, more than half of the respondents viewed the Taliban as "incorruptible," about four out of five considered Taliban adherents to be "brothers" who would stop fighting if they just had jobs, and more than 90 percent felt it would make more sense to negotiate with the Taliban than to continue the fighting.

Compare that with Ambassador Karl Eikenberry's statement to President Obama on November 6, 2009, that President Karzai is "not an adequate partner." Actually, that was an understatement: The man is not just inadequate; he's a negative. I don't think you'll find even 5 percent in Kabul who would call him "incorruptible." (And they're probably on the take.) Our job is made even more difficult because he is such a dismal and counterproductive (alleged) partner.

His arrogance seems boundless. He is so convinced that we are stuck with him that he feels emboldened to threaten to join the Taliban himself. Our actions are partly to blame. Rather than provide our aid through his central government, such as it is, we have to start making end runs around Karzai and deal directly with the tribal leaders at the district and provincial levels. To the extent that we cut him out of the deal, we can prove to the Afghan people that we're not his "enablers." We can offer a "third way," a practical alternative between the Karzai regime's greed and corruption and the Taliban's oppressive medieval rule. With cooperation at the local level, we might be able to bring about a peaceful, smoothly functioning society in which music is allowed, girls can go to school, and towns have clean water and electricity.

Meanwhile, relations with Pakistan, though frequently challenged from different quarters, are better now than at any other time since the low point of September 12, 2001. That's when Deputy Secretary of State Richard Armitage threatened to bomb the country back to the Stone Age if it didn't help us by turning against Al Qaeda and the Taliban. Officially, the Pakistanis did indeed join our side; secretly, they continued to play both ends against the middle, especially through their intelligence agency, the ISI. When we invaded Afghanistan, the Pakistanis provided safe haven to terrorists who fled. There were two reasons for this behavior. First, preparing for when we would eventually leave Afghanistan, they wanted to stay on good terms with the Taliban; that would give them a friendly neighbor to their west, balanced against their dismal relationship with India to the east. Second, they needed the terrorists to become involved in their proxy war with India, especially in Kashmir.

But the monster has turned against its master. Our relations with the Pakistanis have been improving—not because of anything the Obama administration has done but because they've finally acknowledged that they have no control over the Pakistani Taliban. At last, they've seen the light: The most significant danger to the survival of their government and the security of their nuclear weapons is not India, the external threat, but the Pakistani Taliban, the threat right at home.

To be fair, the administration has certainly taken advantage of the Pakistanis' awakening and willingness to work more closely and effectively with America. It is often thanks to good intelligence from Pakistan that our drone strikes are so effective. Currently, we have several hundred Special Operations forces in the country working as advisers and trainers with the Pakistani army. We need more, if the Taliban is to be defeated, but progress is being made.

And there are still gaps in the increasing cooperation. In December 2009, seven of our CIA officers were killed in Khost, Afghanistan, by terrorists in the Haqqani network, which is based in North Waziristan, Pakistan. It was also in North Waziristan that Faisal Shahzad trained with the Pakistani Taliban. It gets more complicated. The Haqqani network is loyal to Mullah Omar, head of the Afghan Taliban. Should not our allies join with us in getting some payback in Waziristan for both the CIA murders and the Times Square attempt? They will not go after the Haqqani network for the simple reason that when we leave Afghanistan, they hope that the Afghan Taliban will return home and oppose Indian influence there. Obama's announcement of a withdrawal date only encourages this kind of thinking. So our former fault lines with Pakistan may be opening again.

Moreover, even as we've been cooperating more with the country in many ways, the various terror groups, unfortunately, have also been cooperating more with one another, sharing resources and capabilities.

Greater numbers of them are engaging in attacks beyond Afghanistan and Pakistan. This greatly troubles Bruce Riedel, who helped formulate President Obama's AfPak strategy and is now a senior fellow at the Saban Center for Middle East Policy:

> The ideology of global jihad has been bought into by more and more militants, even guys who never thought much about the broader world. And this is disturbing because it is a force multiplier for Al Qaeda.

In other words, even as we seem to be getting more help and cooperation from the Pakistani government, we face an increasingly complex challenge.

The Price of Freedom

So based upon what we know, or think we know, what would I say to Rick Rescorla about our handling of the war on terror? That's a conversation that, frankly, I wouldn't want to have right now. I would be ashamed to admit the truth to a man who gave his life protecting those in his care. And that truth is that our government has acted with neither his resolve nor his focus on the task at hand. Our leaders have overestimated the value of political correctness just as they continue to underestimate the nature, motives, tenacity, and capabilities of the enemy. The two misevaluations, I believe, are closely related. At times, it seems that our strongest, most effective defense has been the frequent ineptitude of our enemy. The clock's running out on that strategy.

Remember, the 1993 truck bombing in the World Trade Center was widely derided as an amateurish failure, even though six people were killed. After all, the two towers still stood proud. Rick Rescorla drew a different lesson, and we are in great peril if we cannot follow his example. He redoubled his efforts because he recognized that this was not the end of it but the beginning. Because of his clarity of vision, many families of Morgan Stanley employees were spared the pain of losing a loved one. Will the same be said of the intelligence operatives and other security officials who have been given a lesson, and some valuable breathing room, by the three lone terrorists we've seen in this chapter?

Nearly a decade has gone by since Rick's passing, but the lesson he taught us—and that is still an invaluable teaching tool, if we pay heed—is as important right this moment, as you read, as it was on September 11, 2001. Vigilance is indeed the price of freedom. Preparation is the guarantee of survival.

CHAPTER TEN

When the Bullets Are Real,
There Aren't Any Toy Soldiers

We Need an Effective Military Policy and Strategy

In early February of 2008, I was in the heat of the presidential campaign as one of the few remaining Republicans still in the hunt for the nomination. I had received word from a former cabinet member and staff member that his son, who was a captain in the U.S. Army, had just arrived at Walter Reed Army Medical Center in Washington having been severely wounded in Iraq by an improvised explosive device (IED) and had in fact lost an arm and suffered other serious injuries. I was scheduled to be in Washington a few days later and arranged to visit Captain David Underwood at Walter Reed. I wanted the visit to be personal and private, with no press tagging along or even knowing that I was going. This visit was not a political photo op. It was an opportunity to pay respect and check on the son of a dear friend and colleague, and I hoped to bring some encouragement and appreciation to a true American hero.

As I visited with David that afternoon and watched his wife and children fill his room with their presence and love, I was reminded of the enormous sacrifice our men and women in uniform make on behalf of the rest of us. Though David had lost an arm and would carry shrapnel from a bomb in his legs and body for the rest of his life, here was a soldier who didn't complain of his loss but expressed his gratitude that none of his men had been killed while under his command. These are the men and women who make our country and our world safe and free. We can't do enough for them.

Over two million men and women have served in our armed forces in Iraq and Afghanistan since 9/11. And despite what some on the left might say, they haven't been sent there to fight "culture wars." These are wars fought with real bullets and real bombs. Death, disfigurement, and lifelong disabilities are among the heavy prices paid in the struggle. With so much at stake—and with additional threats no doubt looming around the globe—our soldiers can prevail and survive only by staying focused on their core mission. They should not be relegated to the status of advanced social workers. Those in our military are, of necessity, trained primarily to "kill people and break things"; that's the plan. "Winning hearts and minds," though they can do it well, is a luxury when people are trying to kill them; making friends among the local population is not the main thing when the enemy is paying no attention whatsoever to the traditional rules of engagement or the Geneva Conventions.

Giving Back to Our Veterans

To make their jobs even more difficult, we've stretched our military—both as individuals and as a united fighting force—almost to the breaking point. It is common for a soldier to be assigned two or three tours on the battlefield; four and even five total tours are not all that unusual. Fortunately, Admiral Michael Mullen, chairman of the Joint Chiefs of

Staff, has promised a much-deserved (and saner) new protocol: Soon, our troops will enjoy two years at home for every year served overseas.

Thankfully, he has also addressed the military's past shortcomings in dealing with post-traumatic stress disorder (PTSD) and other mental health issues caused or exacerbated by war experiences. "This is a debt the country owes them for their service," he has said. "It needs to be the first check we write."

Amen to that! A RAND study in 2008 found that about 20 percent of Iraq and Afghanistan vets suffer from either PTSD or depression; worse, a later Stanford University study concluded it was likely closer to 35 percent. Soldiers serving the multiple deployments I mentioned are, according to the *American Journal for Public Health*, three times more likely to suffer from PTSD and depression than those on their first deployment. As I write, the Department of Defense (DOD) is officially listing 35,000 as wounded in action. Add those who suffer mental health problems, however, and the total wounded increases by hundreds of thousands. Almost 20 percent are affected by a traumatic brain injury (TBI) caused by proximity to an explosion. Mental health problems of one sort or another, according to the Department of Veterans Affairs, have been diagnosed in almost 250,000 veterans of the two operations in the Middle East. Of these, tens of thousands have *both* PTSD and TBI.

These statistics, alarming as they are, leave out part of the harsh truth: To this day, despite all of the information available to the public, the stigma of mental health problems is still with us. One result is that too many servicemen and -women are afraid to seek help or talk honestly about their issues; such openness, they fear, will hurt their chances for career advancement inside or outside the military. Perhaps this kind of fear is often justified. All of the press about veterans' mental health issues is a double-edged sword: Important as it is for these problems to be brought to light, wary civilian employers may hesitate to hire the soldiers who are victims. (Vietnam vets had much the same problem after that war, when seemingly every hourlong TV drama and many major high-profile movies featured a soldier home from Nam who, unable to cope with civilian life, eventually went ballistic.)

The military, at least, is trying to avoid the stereotyping within the ranks. The DOD has updated its security clearance application, no longer asking a veteran whether he or she has been treated for mental health issues in the preceding seven years. It's a start.

Homeless Veterans

Not everyone, however, can benefit from such an enlightened approach. For veterans who remain deeply affected, and for their families, the damage caused by severe mental problems can be even more troubling. Mental and neurological problems can result in spousal abuse, divorce, drug and alcohol addiction, homelessness, and suicide. For those reasons, as mandated by the National Defense Authorization Act of 2010, the military now requires confidential, in-person mental health screenings of all troops when they return home. Even so, the military does not have nearly enough medical personnel to provide the necessary mental health treatment, especially for veterans who don't live in or near urban areas.

Veterans of the Iraq and Afghanistan conflicts are at especially high risk for homelessness. Some have portrayed homeless veterans as very likely to have a drug or alcohol problem. In fact, that is often an incorrect stereotype. While some vets are indeed homeless because of service-related mental health issues, including addiction, others are servicewomen who, with their children, have been victimized by foreclosures. Because subprime loans were heavily marketed to military families, the rate of foreclosure in military neighborhoods rose four times faster than the U.S. average rate in 2008. Veterans' advocates are calling for a one-year moratorium before the home of a veteran returning from combat can be put into foreclosure. I think this is a great idea; in fact, it's the least we can do for people who have sacrificed and risked so much for the rest of us.

But not everyone, it seems, is grateful. Sometimes the homes of troops serving abroad have been seized because they were not in residence to comply with the rigid rules of homeowners' associations. If such wrongheaded groups cannot respect the debt they owe to their neighbors in the military, who are protecting their lives, perhaps laws should be enacted to protect their absent neighbors' property rights.

In 2009 the military vowed to end homelessness for veterans of the Iraq and Afghanistan conflicts. As I write, it is estimated that about 130,000 of these men and women remain homeless every night. We definitely have a long way to go.

The System Is a Mess

If you think the government bureaucracy will do a good job of handling your health care (that would be ObamaCare), one look at the VA system will change your mind. The existing system is both extremely frustrating and flagrantly wasteful, as you may know from your own experience or the challenges faced by family and friends. Good care is available, but only after waiting up to six months for the first appointment. Often, veterans must travel great distances to get care. The situation is worse for women than for men; as more women have joined the ranks, the system has not kept up with their needs. In general, processing of claims takes between four months and a year, while appeals of claims take, on average, two years. In the meantime, some vets are so badly injured that they can't work and have no income.

Incredibly, the DOD's and VA's separate systems for health records are not yet fully compatible. Files are lost as veterans move from the

DOD system into the VA. The DOD does not even keep electronic records, now considered an essential component of health records. To fix this mess, all patient records should be electronic and easily transferable between the two departments.

A further complication is that there are two parallel disability benefits systems, each with its own medical examinations and rates of compensation based upon disability ratings. There is a pilot program in place to create a single system, but it has to be expanded nationwide in order to cover all veterans.

Speaking of disability, let's examine the effectiveness of the VA itself. Officials readily admit that almost 20 percent of its disability ratings are *wrong*. It's also true that the outcome of a claim depends heavily on the region where the claim is decided. Believe it or not (considering the time it typically takes to process claims), the VA evaluates claims processors by how quickly they process the paperwork, *not* by the correctness of their decisions. Obviously, claims processors need better training. The VA needs to create a system that values accuracy above all, no matter where the claimant lives.

Not everything is grim for veterans, however. Just as NASA's "race for space" led to the development of our modern world of computer technology, satellite communications, and so much more that we now take for granted, the long recoveries endured by our injured veterans have led to amazing advances in trauma care, burn treatment, and prosthetics. It is never less than heartbreaking to see the injuries of a soldier wounded in ambush or battle. Yet centers like the facial prosthetics lab at Lackland Air Force Base are developing remarkable techniques to ease the wounded patients' transition back to normal life, when possible. "Our goal is to give them the best of the best," says lab director Dr. Joe Villalobos. "We're going to give them the ideal treatment." Our veterans deserve nothing less.

Coming Home: Education and Employment

The title of the Post-9/11 GI Bill, passed in 2008, suggests a creditable program. In fact, an expansion is in order. On the one hand, the benefits to pay for veterans to go to college are excellent, but these checks often arrive very late, leaving the beneficiaries scrambling to pay for tuition, food, and housing. There's just no excuse for that. Also, other worthwhile forms of education, such as vocational schools and Internet-based learning, still aren't covered. They should be.

As for employment, it's proved very tough for veterans to come home from overseas and find themselves smack in the middle of the Great Recession. During 2009, the unemployment rate for Iraq and Afghanistan veterans almost doubled. Let us recognize and praise companies that do the right thing for our veterans by giving them opportunities for employment. And let's offer them tax credits in return, so that other potential employers will be motivated to join in. Congress should be amenable to this idea, since it has already passed the Veterans Employment Opportunities Act, giving veterans preference in hiring for government jobs. Of course (and I hope you're not surprised), it exempted congressional staff jobs—an act so shameful I hope it's been rectified by the time this book reaches print.

Where employment is concerned, too many servicemen and -women don't know their rights, and too many businesses don't understand their obligations under law. The situation is most complicated for National Guardsmen and reservists: According to the Uniformed Services Employment and Reemployment Rights Act, businesses are required to take them back when they return home from a tour of duty, but many employers aren't complying. Some companies refuse to hire them, period, because they don't want the hassle of replacing them if there's another deployment.

A veteran can pursue an employment claim based upon the law, but the burden is on him to prove that he lost the job because of his service. This is backward. The burden should be on the employer to establish a legitimate reason for not taking him back. Yet there's another factor that discourages veterans from making a claim: Incredibly, it can take two years for such employment claims to be resolved.

National Guard and Reserves

In addition to the daunting employment picture for the National Guard and reserves, their overuse in Iraq and Afghanistan has been a tremendous drain on them and their families, their communities, and businesses that would have liked to put them to work. In their civilian lives, a great number of them protect us as our police, firefighters, and paramedics. But since 9/11, as you may be amazed to read, there have been times when almost half of our combat troops in Iraq and more than half of those in Afghanistan have been either National Guard or reserves.

I saw this firsthand during my ten-and-a-half-year tenure as a governor, which included serving as commander in chief of our eleven thousand men and women of the Army and Air Force National Guard. Repeated deployments to Iraq, Afghanistan, and domestic duty, such as helping out in the aftermath of Katrina, wore heavily not only on the guard personnel but also on their families and employers.

Forgive me for bragging here about my guardsmen, but I'm going to anyway. The 39th Brigade of the Arkansas Guard were actually the first National Guard troops to make it to New Orleans from outside Louisiana. Later, when General Steven Blum, chief of the National Guard Bureau, and I were on a flight to Iraq, he told me a terrific story about the timing of their arrival. He was being quizzed by President

Bush at the Katrina national command center in Texas as to when the guard would get to New Orleans. Then, at that very moment, the TV screen showed the 39th rolling into town. "There they are, Mr. President!" the relieved general shouted. When he told me the story, he said, "I will always love your guys from the 39th!"

As that event proved, we need our National Guard at home for emergencies. Did you know that at the time of Hurricane Katrina a third of the Louisiana and Mississippi National Guard were serving in Iraq or Afghanistan? This is insane, since they're the go-to guys when disaster strikes: hurricanes, floods, wildfires, tornadoes, ice storms, earthquakes, and man-made catastrophes like the horrendous BP oil deluge. Naturally, when large numbers of the guard are overseas, our governors are less able to respond to a crisis quickly and effectively. Getting help from other states eats up precious time and requires lots of red tape. (Oh, I forgot.... There's always the White House to provide a timely and worthwhile response!) Yet thank the Lord, there does exist an avenue that most people are not aware of: a very useful, efficient system known as the Emergency Management Assistance Compact (EMAC). EMAC allows governors to share assets with other states on a moment's notice without the endless, time-consuming nonsense that so often slows things down when the federal bureaucracy is involved. Governors know that EMAC, though almost never mentioned in the media, is effective, quick, and responsive. It can make the difference between life-saving response and failure.

By the way, when our guardsmen are deployed overseas, their equipment goes with them. Much of it—including items you'd think we just might need sometime back home, such as helicopters and trucks—somehow gets left over there. So these tours of duty deprive states of both the personnel and the equipment required for emergencies. And without the latter, we can't even train new recruits.

Finally, there's one more reason to keep our National Guard here, and that's law enforcement, particularly along our troubled border with Mexico. It is the law, by the way, that our active-duty military and our reserves cannot participate in actions there.

What Is Our Mission?

"We'll know it when we see it" may work as a definition of pornography, as a Supreme Court justice once suggested, but not as a definition of victory in a war. And if we don't know the precise end our military is trying to achieve, we can't focus on the means to achieve it.

For example, in both Iraq and Afghanistan, we've been following the strategy of "clear, hold, and build." In other words, we do it all! That is a dangerous lack of focus. Instead, the goal given to our troops should be to clear the enemy from targeted territory—just that alone. Next, the host country's troops and police should hold that cleared territory while civilians build, or rebuild, its infrastructure and institutions. To put it bluntly, we've had too many of our troops spending too much of their time painting schools and digging wells. They should be allowed to focus on killing Islamic extremists who want us all to die.

Because of this scattershot, imprecise mission, a small group of Americans has borne the brunt of these wars by deploying again and again. The problem is that the DOD is calling on them to do tasks that should instead be undertaken by U.S. civilian agencies and our NATO allies.

As the former top commander of our forces in Afghanistan and a retired army general, Ambassador Eikenberry is in a unique position to know exactly what our military should and should not be doing. For that reason, he's asked for more civilian personnel so that our troops can concentrate on their military mission, but he's so far received only about one civilian expert for every hundred troops—nowhere near what he needs. To carry out the many nonmilitary goals of the war in Afghanistan, the DOD needs more support from the State Department, the U.S. Agency for International Development, the Department of Agriculture, the Justice Department, the Drug Enforcement Agency, and the Department of Homeland Security.

We could also use much more military support from our NATO allies, but most have shown an aversion to combat. Most of the fighting is in southern Afghanistan, but both France and Germany have been unwilling to go there. (Think there's a connection? Oui, oui!) Okay, if NATO won't send or effectively deploy combat troops, let it contribute to stabilizing the country by at least sending more personnel to help with training the police, building infrastructure, and establishing civilian institutions. Then we can get back to the dirty work of fighting and defeating terrorists.

Don't Ask, Don't Tell ... Don't Serve

Under the Obama administration, the question of whether or not openly gay men and women should be able to serve in the military has become one of the hot topics of the day. I have asked numerous military men and women ranging in rank from generals to fresh recruits what they thought about this very controversial and divisive issue, but the real question to be answered is what's in the best interest of the military mission. The military is not about individual preferences but about cohesion of the unit. Let me attempt to address this controversy and shed some light on the likely impact of any policy change.

In 1993 Congress affirmed that the unit comes before the individual, passing legislation that argued "[since] military life is fundamentally different from civilian life" and imposes "little or no privacy," homosexuals cannot be allowed to serve. If they were, they would create "an unacceptable risk to the high standards of morale, good order and discipline, and unit cohesion that are the essence of military capability."

But President Clinton contradicted that law by introducing the absurd concept of "Don't Ask, Don't Tell" (DADT), which President Obama now wants to rescind. Before you applaud, understand that he does not intend to overturn a policy that allows for the recruitment of homosexual soldiers but rather to let them serve openly rather than (as now) discreetly. His aim cannot possibly be to strengthen our military, because it would do just the opposite: create unnecessary tensions, divisions, and stress among men and women who must depend on one another in order to survive. His motivation is purely political, a ploy to strengthen his support from the left. This is the liberal "core" that has been disappointed with him because they expected him to cut and run from Iraq and Afghanistan and close the terrorist prison at Guantanamo. In other words, he is using our servicemen and servicewomen as pawns in shoring up his political base.

In a 2008 *Military Times* poll of active-duty servicemen and women, 10 percent said they would leave the military if homosexuals were allowed to serve openly; an additional 14 percent said they would consider doing so. That adds up to a quarter of our military forces! One recently retired general has said, "I joined the military when homosexuality was illegal, I served when it was allowed, and I have decided to retire before it was required." If a wave of resignations hit a private company, if middle and senior managers left in a body, the solution would be to recruit from other companies. But if our career officers and enlisted men walked away, where would we find their replacements? Would the liberal cast of characters in Washington who support this change rush right down to the recruitment office? I don't think so!

Not surprisingly, conservatives are considerably more likely to join the military than liberals are. In other words, liberal elitists are seeking to impose their will and values upon an institution their like seldom choose as a career and thus don't really understand. This is dangerous arrogance. It would threaten the very existence of our volunteer military if they succeed in creating conditions that discourage social conservatives from volunteering, since such conservatives are more likely than liberals to object to serving alongside soldiers who are openly homosexual. Those who advocate the same-sex agenda should consider the many potential costs, including the possible need to reinstate the draft.

Lest you think I'm stereotyping conservative views, a June 2010 *USA Today*/Gallup poll found that 48 percent of conservatives describe themselves as "extremely patriotic," compared to only 19 percent of liberals and 22 percent of Americans ages eighteen to twenty-nine. If about 80 percent of liberals in general and young people in particular aren't patriotic enough to volunteer for the military, then good luck replacing all those conservatives leaving the ranks.

In contrast with the likelihood of resignations if the current policy is overturned, note that over the past decades, discharges for homosexuality have been less than one-half of 1 percent of all discharges. Furthermore, many of these have been for actual sexual assaults, not for just "telling." This pattern has not been a significant loss compared with the sweeping losses that would result from changing the policy.

Jumping the Gun

As we've seen before, this administration sure seems to enjoy taking action before all the facts are in! Like the Red Queen in *Alice in Wonderland*, who said, "Sentence first, verdict afterward!" they do things backward. (The operative motto of Congress is only slightly different: "Pass first, read afterward!") In this case, it was wrong of the House to vote to repeal DADT—a major policy change by any standards—before the military finished its own internal review. Admiral Mullen publicly made just that point. Moreover, the House vote, as a done deal, is likely to discourage honest input from the ranks.

Most important, the final decision isn't even Congress's to make. President Obama gets the last word (yes, yes, I know), in consultation with Secretary Gates and Admiral Mullen. When the decision is made, I can only hope that our commander in chief will step back from the front lines of his ongoing "culture war" and instead dedicate himself to the task of ensuring that our armed forces are as strong and united as possible. Essential to that job is keeping our servicemen and servicewomen as safe as they can be, without the distractions to unit cohesion that can be caused by a leftist political agenda.

CHAPTER ELEVEN

With Enemies Like This, Who Needs Friends?

We Need to Strengthen America's Position on the World Stage

I've spent most of this book discussing the problems we face at home, but I want to take a moment to say that in order for America to be as great as it possibly can be, we must remember our place in the world. Most of us live our lives not thinking about what's going on in some other country. Trying to cover the cost of rent, groceries, and gas for the car doesn't afford us the luxury of spending much time pondering what they are thinking in Pakistan. But dealing with friends and enemies in the world community is important, and much of our own national security is at stake.

Nothing presents a more tangled Gordian knot for a new president than foreign policy. Indeed, much of Barack Obama's case for electing him hinged on convincing voters that President Bush's approach of staunchly standing by our allies and standing up to our enemies was too simplistic and that a sophisticated, "nuanced" approach to dealing with the world would make nations that dreamed of killing us suddenly love us enough to want to take us to the prom. The Left even gave this approach an appropriately egotistical name: "smart diplomacy."

As if the only reason there were intractable problems in the world was that the diplomats who had dealt with them through the previous decades were morons compared to Obama's Ivy League brain trust. It's like the kid in school who waves his *A* test score in front of the entire class but never gets picked to play baseball. He's an arrogant nerd, and no matter how smart he is, he can't hit, he can't throw, and he can't run.

As of this writing, the nuance brigade have been applying their superior intellects to American foreign policy for approximately eighteen months, and there's no question that they've had a major impact on our standing in the world. Tin-pot dictators from the Middle East to Latin American to North Korea still hate us; only now they openly mock us as well, defying American threats like a spoiled child who knows that no matter how much his parents threaten, they'll never really spank him. British leaders question whether our two nations' time-tested "special relationship" has been irreparably shredded. Some of our bravest allies in Eastern Europe feel betrayed at seeing the promise of an American missile shield blithely broken to appease Russian hard-liners. And the war in Afghanistan has been simultaneously escalated and muddled. The administration attempted to cover every bet by increasing troop levels while announcing its timetable for leaving. There's no greater gift to an enemy in wartime than to reveal when you plan to stop fighting. The result: more combat-related deaths in the first eighteen months of Obama's tenure than in the previous nine years of war. Obama's handpicked commander was even forced to resign after a *Rolling Stone* writer quoted him openly disparaging the competence of his superiors.

The one bright spot: Among nations that are traditionally anti-American, President Obama still enjoys high approval ratings. Why am I not surprised?

We Must Remember Our History to Improve Our Future

One of the first things President Obama did upon assuming office was to return the bust of Winston Churchill that the British government had presented to President Bush right after 9/11, on indefinite loan from their national art collection. This didn't just insult our closest ally; it insulted all Americans. We like Winston Churchill and were proud to have that bust in the Oval Office as a reminder of British solidarity with us, from the First and Second World Wars through the war on terror. Obama's action wasn't just boorish; it set an ominous tone for what was to come. What else was going to be tossed out that we liked and believed in but that this new president didn't?

The British newspaper the *Daily Telegraph* explained Obama's strange behavior: "Churchill has less happy connotations for Mr. Obama than for those American politicians who celebrate his wartime leadership. It was during Churchill's second premiership that Britain suppressed Kenya's Mau Mau rebellion. . . . Kenyans allegedly tortured by the colonial regime included one Hussein Onyango Obama, the President's grandfather."

Every president is the keeper of our American narrative, "our story." He is the commander in chief, yes, but he is also commemorator in chief. Our wartime partnership with Winston Churchill and the British people is part of our story; the Mau Mau rebellion is not. When we elect a president, we entrust to him not just our security but also our story. The two are inseparable because our security depends on the story that we believe in, that inspires us, that we teach our children, and that we, as a nation, are willing to fight for.

President Obama's emphasis on *his* story rather than *history* has become symptomatic of his tenure. He is going to impose his agenda on Americans, and he doesn't care if we don't share it, don't believe in it, or don't want it.

In his Cairo address of June 2009, President Obama declared, "Any world order that elevates one nation or group of people over another will inevitably fail." He used very similar language before the UN General Assembly in September 2009: "No one nation can or should try to dominate another nation. No world order that elevates one nation or group of people over another will succeed."

This is a startling and disturbing view of America. Here again, he rejects a vital part of our story: our shared belief in American exceptionalism. By the time the French writer Alexis de Tocqueville coined that phrase in 1831, it had already been part of our national psyche for two hundred years, going all the way back to John Winthrop's 1630 speech to the Puritans he led:

> For we must consider that we shall be as a City upon a
> hill. The eyes of all people are upon us. So that if we shall
> deal falsely with our God in the work we have undertaken,
> and so cause Him to withdraw His present help from us, we
> shall be made a story and a byword throughout the world.

For almost four hundred years now, Americans have understood that we have been chosen for greatness but have heavy responsibilities. Yet President Obama takes what we regard as a solemn covenant and reduces it to silly chauvinism, as he did in an interview in Strasbourg in April 2009: "I believe in American exceptionalism, just as I suspect that the Brits believe in British exceptionalism and the Greeks believe in Greek exceptionalism." So according to him, America is just one nation among many, and we haven't achieved and don't stand for anything special. Then why is America the only nation with such a staggering illegal immigration problem? When other nations put walls and guards on their borders, it's to keep people from leaving; when we do so, it's to keep them from flooding in.

In May 2010, the president presented his first National Security Strategy (NSS), a document the president is required to send Congress every four years. President Obama's introductory letter doesn't sound as if it comes from the leader of the world's only superpower. "Our long-term security will come not from our ability to instill fear in other peoples." *Since when?* If that's true, why bother spending seven hundred billion dollars a year on our military? Theodore Roosevelt believed that the way to command the world's respect was to "speak softly and carry a big stick." Other presidents have chosen to speak loudly and carry a big stick. But this is the first president who believes you can command the respect of rogue nations by apologizing and throwing away the stick.

With respect to Iran, the NSS is truly pathetic: "Yet if the Iranian Government continues to refuse to live up to its international obligations, it will face greater isolation." You can almost hear the laughter all the way from Tehran. Isolation? That's our threat? "Do as we say, or we'll make you unpopular?" Well, it's certainly consistent with not wanting to instill fear in anyone. And just look at how well it's worked on North Korea.

The Obama NSS backs away from the Bush doctrine's post-9/11 assertion of our right to wage a preemptive war in our defense. Instead, it is big on multilateral pie in the sky: "We must focus American engagement on strengthening international institutions and galvanizing the collective action that can serve common interests." And because we all know what a ringing success the UN has been, "we are enhancing our coordination with the U.N. and its agencies." In other words, we are going to waste a lot of time and money and get nothing in return that enhances our security.

Obama is naive both in what he thinks he can accomplish and in where he believes our interests lie, and he harbors far too much faith in the power of his own personality to change the tides of history, just as he once promised that it would lower the tides of the oceans. For instance, he asserts that his "biography" gives him credibility in the Muslim world. But from their point of view, he is someone who was born Muslim through his father and converted to Christianity. Abandoning your faith doesn't win you the "Mr. Popularity" title in the Muslim world.

Israel: Our Ally in a Sea of Enemies

President Obama has suggested that Israelis are suspicious of him because his middle name is Hussein. Yes, I'm sure that's it. The fact that he has abandoned decades of bipartisan U.S. policy toward Israel has nothing to do with it! In June 2010, the Israeli ambassador to the United States, Michael Oren, lamented Obama's stunning policy shifts as "a tectonic rift in which continents are drifting apart." These shifts are not just strategically wrongheaded; they are morally repugnant.

President Obama views Israel not as the partner and ally in the war on terror that she is, but as part of the problem, if not the root of it. The truth is that radical Islam is the problem, and Obama's consistent refusal to call that evil by its true name will never change that fact.

In his Cairo address of June 2009, President Obama said, "Islam is not part of the problem in combating violent extremism—it is an important part of promoting peace." Then why don't moderate Muslims rise up and do more to defeat the radicals among them? The extremists get much of their funding and other support with a wink and nod from those who claim to be moderates. Besides all the self-proclaimed wolves in the Muslim world, there are far too many wolves in sheep's clothing, saying one thing and doing another. The president doesn't see our allies and our enemies clearly because he doesn't see the world clearly. Again, the haze of nuance obscures the simple truth.

Terrorists like Al Qaeda, the Taliban, Hamas, and Hezbollah, and state sponsors of terror like Iran, aren't just against the Jews. They are against everyone who doesn't subscribe to their own narrow, extremist version of Islam—Christians, Hindus, Buddhists, atheists, even all other Muslims. The Muslim world must deal with its repressive, corrupt regimes; its failed states that can't provide the most basic services to their people; its systemic culture of poverty, illiteracy, and injustice; and all its tribal, ethnic, and religious rivalries. Israel has nothing to do with any of this.

If Israel didn't exist, would India and Pakistan suddenly be friends? Would the Pashtuns, Tajiks, and Uzbeks in Afghanistan get along? Would the Sunni Arab states not feel threatened by the non-Arab Persian Shiites of Iran; would the Salafi and Zaydi sects in Yemen suddenly agree on religious doctrine? Would all the ancient and endless Hatfield-and-McCoy tribal disputes that define that part of the world end? Of course not. Osama bin Laden would still want to destroy us and our way of life, would still want to establish a worldwide caliphate taking us back to the "good old days" of 1,400 years ago.

President Obama has declared that achieving peace between Israel and the Palestinians is a vital national-security interest of the United States. I believe we best pursue our national security by staying out of it, other than to provide Israel all the moral and military support she needs and deserves. Quite frankly, until Hamas recognizes Israel's right to exist, renounces violence, and accepts previous agreements, there's really nothing that can be done and no point in pressuring Israel to do it anyway.

Our national-security interest lies in standing with our friends in the fight against Islamic terror. Distancing ourselves from Israel contradicts that interest, emboldening our mutual enemies, making Israel feel even more threatened and isolated, and causing our other friends to wonder who will be thrown under the bus next. To the Arab/Muslim world, such distancing is a sign of American weakness and Israeli vulnerability that only encourages them to double down on their genocidal plans for Israel.

Both European and Muslim countries look to us to see how far they can take their Israel bashing. President Obama has sent out signals—very dangerous signals—that say, "Go ahead and bash Israel all you want, literally and figuratively, fine with us."

As a candidate, President Obama never told the American people that he would order a draconian freeze on all Israeli settlement activity, with no exceptions. He never told us that he would repudiate the understanding by Presidents Clinton and Bush that Israel would never give up all settlements but would keep some close to the 1949 armistice line by swapping land. In fact, his call for a complete freeze contradicted the policy of all U. S. presidents since Israel's victory in the 1967 war. How absurd is it for the U.S. government to tell an Israeli family that they can't add a nursery to their home to welcome a new baby or tell an Israeli village that they can't add a classroom to their schoolhouse?

But after his first meeting with Prime Minister Benjamin Netanyahu in May 2009, President Obama announced, "Settlements have to be stopped in order for us to move forward." With whom were the Israelis supposed to move forward? With the Hamas terrorists of the Gaza Strip? With Fatah's Mahmoud Abbas, who barely controls the sidewalk in front of his office in the West Bank? Yet Obama took the ball out of the Palestinians' court and said that it wasn't their wanton *destruction* of life and property that was holding back the peace process. No, it was Israeli *construction*.

Moreover, when President Obama announced his new settlement policy, he coupled it with an implied threat that unless the Israelis capitulated, he might retaliate by not doing as much as he could to stop

Iran from getting nuclear weapons. He sounded ominously like Tony Soprano.

President Obama used identical "blame the victim" language in both his Cairo address of June 2009 and his address to the UN General Assembly in September 2009, saying that the United States "does not accept the legitimacy of continued Israeli settlements." *Legitimacy* was an odd choice of words, considering how few people in his audience even accepted the legitimacy of Israel's existence.

In March 2010, while Vice President Biden was visiting Israel, President Obama found the flimsy pretext he had been looking for to show the world how tough he could be on Israel without any justification or provocation by the Israelis other than doing what any sovereign country could be expected to do.

What was the terrible outrage that occurred during that visit? Brace yourself. A midlevel bureaucrat moved along the approval process for some apartments in an existing Jewish neighborhood in East Jerusalem. It obviously had nothing to do with Israel's honoring of its construction freeze in the West Bank and was in keeping with Israeli policies under every prime minister since the reunification of Jerusalem after Israel's neighbors attacked her in 1967. Those policies had not deterred the Egyptians and Jordanians from signing peace treaties with Israel.

But later that month, President Obama inflated that incident into an excuse to humiliate Prime Minister Netanyahu on his visit to the White House, refusing to be photographed with him or hold a joint press conference or issue a joint statement. Obama even scheduled the meeting to run until dinnertime and then ostentatiously announced he was going to eat without inviting his guest to join him. No soup for you!

Skip forward to May 2010: At the nuclear nonproliferation treaty (NPT) conference, the United States for the first time caved in to an Arab demand that Israel be singled out for not signing the NPT. The whole world knows that Israel has nuclear weapons, so this posturing was pure political theater. The final resolution didn't mention either Pakistan or India, which also have nuclear weapons and haven't signed the NPT, or Iran, which has signed but whose nuclear program is in defiance of the treaty.

Preventing specific mention of Israel had been official U.S. policy since 1969. In fact, it had been President Obama's policy in his September 2009 address to the UN General Assembly, where he said regarding the NPT, "Let me be clear, this is not about singling out individual nations." So he didn't just go back on the word of previous American presidents; he went back on his own word given before the whole world.

Having signed this document, the Obama administration then issued a statement that it "deplores the decision to single out Israel." Why on earth would we *ever* sign a document that we deplore? What sort of amateur, incoherent policy is this?

On May 31, 2010, a flotilla of troublemakers with terrorist links set out from Turkey to break Israel's naval blockade of Gaza. The blockade is entirely legal and enforceable under international law. Since Israel's withdrawal from Gaza, Hamas has fired over four thousand rockets at Israeli civilians. Allowing weapons deliveries to Hamas via ship would make mass murder as convenient as buying DVDs on Amazon.com. This is why Israel was completely justified in taking action to stop the deliberate violation of the blockade.

After that deadly incident, the United States approved a statement by the president of the UN Security Council that, predictably, criticized Israel for defending herself. Such a statement must be unanimous, so the United States could have easily stopped it but didn't. Yet if it weren't for President Obama's policy reversals, which encouraged the provocateurs to challenge the blockade, the incident probably never would have happened.

Elliott Abrams, who held senior foreign-policy positions under

Presidents Reagan and Bush 43, wrote that President Obama "abandoned Israel in the U.N. and in the NPT conference in the course of one week. . . . The White House does not wish to stand with Israel against the mob because it does not have a policy of solidarity with Israel. Rather, its policy is one of distancing and pressure."

The United States and Israel are fighting the same bad guys—Hamas, Hezbollah, Al Qaeda, the Taliban, Iran. To tie this complicated bundle of issues into one simple question, how does turning against our friend, and siding with our common enemies, strengthen national security and help us win the war on terror?

Iran

President Obama clearly understands the gift of time. After all, he has said that he sent more troops to Afghanistan "to provide the time and the space for the Afghan government to build up its security capacities." It makes sense to give the gift of time to our ally, but why do the same for our enemy? Obama has repeatedly given Iran the gift it most wants and needs from us: the gift of time to produce nuclear weapons.

The president spent months negotiating sanctions, weakening what we originally wanted by making major concessions to Russia and China, until he got another round through the Security Council on June 9, 2010. As of this writing, we're up to round four and counting (didn't Einstein define insanity as doing the same thing over and over again and expecting a different result?). Russia and China didn't agree to anything they're not certain Iran can weasel around, just as it has all the previous sanctions, or to anything that threatens their own interests. We did not impose any restrictions on China's growing investments in Iran's oil and natural-gas sectors.

Russia can still sell its S-300 antiaircraft missiles, which would make it more dangerous for the United States or Israel to attack Iranian nuclear installations. We also agreed to abandon existing sanctions against Russian companies that worked on Iran's nuclear and ballistic missile programs and made illegal arms sales to Syria.

John Bolton, President George W. Bush's UN ambassador, said that Russian foreign minister Sergei Lavrov "sensed desperation in the Obama administration on this Iran resolution and probably extracted all that the traffic would bear." And David Kramer, who ran Russian policy at the State Department in the Bush administration, commented, "Let's not forget that Russia supported three previous resolutions [under President Bush] and didn't get 'rewarded' for those votes."

The bottom line, after all that effort and spending of diplomatic capital? Asked about the latest sanctions, CIA director Leon Panetta replied, "Will it deter [Iran] from their ambitions with regards to nuclear capability? Probably not." He also said that Iran now has enough material for two nuclear bombs. The immediate threat isn't a nuclear weapon on a missile, although Iran will get to that point soon enough, but one placed on a truck for its terrorist friends, Hamas or Hezbollah.

President Obama has been so anxious to negotiate with an Iranian government that has no interest in dealing with him and did not respond with affection to his two love letters that he shamefully held his tongue when Green Movement prodemocracy forces protested the rigged election in June 2009. This is the man who told the graduating class at West Point in May 2010, "America will always seek a world that extends these rights, so that when an individual is being silenced, we aim to be her voice." But he provided barely a whisper of support to protesters who were risking their lives to make their own voices heard. Iranians who believed in the exceptionalism of American-style freedom, like the martyred protester Neda Agha-Soltan, were beaten and murdered, while the tyrants in Tehran once again thumbed their noses at Washington.

How did the respect America engendered in its allies and the fear it inspired in its enemies crumble away so quickly? At the risk of being labeled simplistic, I would suggest that it was nuked by nuance. A vac-illating foreign policy convinced our allies that we couldn't be trusted and our enemies that we need not be feared. An administration besot-ted with its own moral and intellectual superiority believed that a will-ingness to criticize America's friends and see the viewpoint of its enemies was a sign of their own advanced intellectual flexibility, their "smart diplomacy." Their egos couldn't let them accept that perhaps their unenlightened predecessors had been right all along and that the simplest maxims really are correct: Freedom is better than oppression. Democracy is morally superior to dictatorships. You don't stab your friends in the back. Bullies aren't impressed by weakness. And often-times, the only way to prevent war is to convince your enemies that you are ready, willing, and able to fight one.

CHAPTER TWELVE

Hope Is More Than Just
the Name of My Hometown

We Need to Have Faith in the Future,
No Matter How Big Our Present Problems Are

I was born and raised in Hope, Arkansas, but to me that name means more than just my hometown; it embodies the attitude I have about America today. I've spent most of this book discussing a lot of big, important, and urgent issues (which I think is appropriate for a book about government). But in this last chapter I want to share some intensely personal observations and also give you a glimpse of things I've been doing since my last book.

Despite the numerous problems and challenges I've talked about here, I believe that far too many people are guilty of hand-wringing, worry, and despair over the future of America. That's not my theme. Some people have seen the rise of the Tea Party movement as an indication that our country is dangerously lost . . . that our time as a strong, unified nation will soon be over.

I think it's just the opposite: To me, the uprising of ordinary citizens in this movement is in fact an affirmation of everything that is wonderful and positive about America. This country was brilliantly designed by its founders to be a kind of giant self-cleaning oven. When things gunk up the parts and dirty up the works, it's time to turn on the self-cleaning function. What happens then, as you probably know, is that the heat is raised to a level above any temperature ever used for cooking. All of the dross of leftover food and debris is turned into charred ashes. The oven door is opened; that which remains is easily wiped clean.

In essence, the uprising of the Tea Party movement is America's affirmation that it is functioning as it was intended to function. The system is creatively at work because it is self-correcting government excesses, loss of control, and isolation from the real needs of the people.

Americans should not fear these movements as indicating the end. Rather, these are indications of a profound and positive rebirth. I have chosen to disable the gloom-and-doom buttons on the dashboard of my life because I believe it is far more important to see where we are going than to remain focused on where we are. As a Christian believer, I have a deep-rooted optimism based on the fact that even if the country should fail, God's kingdom will not.

Christian believers in this country essentially carry two passports. One is their temporal passport of U.S. citizenship; the other is their eternal passport to eternal life. We are dual citizens of both earth and heaven. While we can hope that both of these kingdoms will survive and sustain, we know for certain that ultimately the kingdom of heaven will survive and sustain.

This confidence is somewhat similar to the experience I've had watching basketball games on tape delay. Several years ago, when the Arkansas Razorbacks were at the peak of the NCAA success that culminated in their winning the 1994 national championship, the local ABC affiliate in Little Rock, KATB-TV, was not able to obtain live broadcast rights for every game. They'd have to tape some games live, then play them back in their entirety after the 10:00 P.M. news. In order to give the viewer a sense of live action, the sportscaster would encourage those who planned to watch the game to turn down the volume on their TV sets when he read the final score on the air. That way, even though the game was over and the final score determined, those who wanted to stay up late and watch it would not know the outcome until the end. But I never understood why anyone would stay up until 1:00 A.M. watching a taped game without taking advantage of the obtainable knowledge about the final score. I never considered turning down the volume during the sportscast, because I wanted to know the outcome. If the Razorbacks had won, I'd pop some popcorn, put my feet up, and confidently watch the ballgame. Even in the most intense moments, when the Hogs would fall behind, I was never worried: I knew victory was assured. Even if they were down seven points in the last minute of play, I was confident. If anyone else was up, I could tell them not to worry: "They are going to do fine." And of course they did.

Christian believers who have read to the end of the Bible have the confidence that, no matter how challenging things can be, the ultimate outcome will be positive and victorious. That's one reason, among many, that there should be no gloom and doom in the mind, heart, or spirit of a true believer.

Boundary Stones

Even if you are not a believer, here's some reasoning you might agree with from Proverbs 22:28: "Remove not the ancient landmark which your fathers have set." The verse refers to ancient boundary stones, which were not to be moved because they served as navigation points— the GPS of biblical times. If they were moved, travelers who depended on them might become hopelessly lost, perhaps in an otherwise featureless desert or dangerous mountainous terrain.

Our culture has inherited invaluable political boundary stones from the Founding Fathers. Any culture in which people move the abiding boundary stones of civilization risks becoming lost, confused, and disoriented. What looks to many of us like a great deal of confusion and darkness in America today is the result of moving cultural boundary stones.

We have moved the boundary stones of freedom and, by trading individual liberty for government dependency, no longer find our pathways to knowledge of the true meaning of liberty.

We have moved the boundary stones of marriage by opening the doors to no-fault divorce, making it easier to get out of a marriage than to get out of a contract for purchase of a used car.

We have moved the boundary stones of family by having some judges and some state legislatures redefine what marriage means, thus abandoning the time-tested definition of one man and one woman in a relationship for life to new definitions, such as legalized relationships between two men, two women, or an individual with two or more partners.

The degree to which we move the boundary stones that form our political legacy, as well as other moral, ethical, and spiritual navigation points, is the degree to which our society, culture, country, and civilization will begin to lose their way and eventually become hopelessly lost.

On the Road Again

But as I've said, I'm basically an optimist. Part of the reason is that I'm lucky enough to have contact with so many of you as I travel around the country, sometimes on a book tour, often to make political or inspirational speeches, and, increasingly, wherever I am, remaining in touch with the American reality in my new broadcasting career.

My life has changed dramatically. As governor, on any given day I might experience a tornado that would completely upend my schedule and other priorities. Especially the one on March 1, 1997, which ripped through almost 250 miles from the southwest corner of the state to the northeast corner in what was eventually a series of over twenty tornadoes that killed thirty people and caused millions of dollars in damage. Likewise, a tornado on January 21, 1999, swept through a number of counties, killing twenty-seven people, including one not five hundred yards from the front door of the governor's mansion, and devastating the neighborhood around us. And on top of all of the natural disasters, our state also had to confront some man-made catastrophes as well, like the 1998 school shooting at Westside Middle School in Jonesboro.

Now the challenges I face in my life are almost completely different, requiring that I balance what for me are several virtually separate universes. My daily radio commentaries, the *Huckabee Report*, could stand alone as a full-time endeavor. In addition, I'm engaged in the process of putting together my weekly Fox News channel TV show, which is viewed on Saturdays and Sundays by a larger audience than all the other Cablevision news channels combined in that time slot. (In fact, in most cases, it remains the top-rated weekend show in all of cable news.) In addition to those two highly visible media endeavors, I speak as many as fourteen times a month to various corporate groups, trade associations, conventions, and nonprofit organizations. I'm also involved in ongoing writing projects, such as this book, and am directly involved in the operation and management of my political organization, Huck PAC, even though I receive no compensation whatsoever for my involvement with its endeavors to elect conservative candidates to public office.

Some of you may find it ironic that I'm so deeply engaged in media activities, since I have so openly and frankly criticized some aspects of press coverage over the years. I still sometimes fear that our political system is increasingly dominated by the short attention span that is aggravated by the twenty-four-hour cable news channels, bloggers, and Internet news services. Often they are more interested in being first than in being right and more interested in getting ratings or Web site hits than in getting the solid facts. This overwhelming change in the way most people get news has produced unwritten new rules that really should be taught to every student coming into our education system.

A generation ago, a person might have obtained his news from the newspaper on the doorstep or from one of three national TV network evening newscasts. Here's the critically important thing: Before that news was delivered to the end user, the consumer, it had not only been gathered by a reporter but most likely also fact-checked by an editor and gone over repeatedly by copy editors and others checking not only for grammatical errors but also for factual veracity. Now fast-forward to today, when people get much of their news from their smart phones, the Internet, or some other form of new media. Now each end user, each consumer, must become his or her own editor. There is no longer likely to be a thorough review process between the gatherer/reporter of news and the consumer of news. Anyone who accepts purported fact at face value is likely to be duped by wily, inaccurate, or, at best, misleading declarations. That's the downside, but the upside of the new media is that more information is available from a much greater variety of sources; one has the opportunity to access vast amounts of data and information. In the best-case scenario, the careful, thoughtful consumer can become better informed and perhaps draw individual conclusions that have not been filtered by a newspaper editor or broadcast news director.

Some of the benefits of the new technology are certainly helpful to me in a personal way. The *Huckabee Report*—which I record three times a day, five days a week, for broadcast on nearly six hundred radio stations—would not have been possible fifteen or twenty years ago. I would have been required to go to a local radio station or other production facility for each commentary, which would then have been transmitted to the network for national distribution. This would have been impossible given the intensity of my travel schedule. Today's *Huckabee Report* is made possible almost entirely because of the capacity of the Internet. I carry with me wherever I travel the compact equipment that allows me to broadcast instantly.

Here's how it works. Each day I consult with writers, based in Dallas, who prepare a compilation of news reports and features gathered, literally, from news sources around the world. Once I receive the material over the Net, I edit it, add some personal touches and commentary and perspective, assemble the stories in order to time them, sort them, and piece them together to create the exact to-the-second program that will become that day's *Huckabee Report*. My portable equipment allows me to record the program into my MacBook, convert the audio into an MP3 file, then upload it to an engineer at Citadel Broadcasting by way of the Internet. He packages the program for broadcast before uploading it—also on the Internet—to the network headquarters in New York for distribution to the nearly six hundred stations. In other words, every hotel room I stay in becomes my studio, as does my home office or wherever I happen to be. I am literally able to do the *Huckabee Report* from anywhere in the world where there is an Internet connection available. I've done reports from Japan, Korea, Israel, Ireland, France, Italy, and the Virgin Islands, as well as most of the fifty states. The technology is not only convenient; it also allows me to travel continually, getting the perspectives of locales and individuals across the spectrum of American and international life. It's far better to offer a perspective that is informed by actually touching and talking to people every day than to pontificate from a sterile studio environment, where my perspective might be filtered from traditional news sources.

What's It Really Like There?

I'm often asked—in fact, on a daily basis—about the working atmosphere at Fox News channel. Thankfully, I can truthfully answer that the atmosphere there is extraordinarily collegial. In fact, it is a unique environment for a media company, given the typical backbiting, dog-eat-dog behaviors at many ego-driven broadcasting centers. While there is a strong ambition within the Fox News channel family to excel and achieve high ratings and success, there is a surprisingly positive working relationship among the team. I attribute much of this to Roger Ailes, who is not only a media visionary but also a person who goes out of his way to encourage all of us to bring our best game to the field. He keeps us all mindful that the competition is fierce but not internal. His penchant for spotting and developing exceptional talent is obvious from the stunning and continually soaring success of Fox News.

One thing that I find surprises many people about Fox is the wall of separation between the news division and the program division. Critics of the company point to program hosts/commentators like Bill O'Reilly, Sean Hannity, Glenn Beck, or me as being partisan or at least decidedly philosophical and ideological. What such critics miss is that the programs that are clearly labeled and carried out as commentary make no apology or pretense about having a strongly stated point of view. On the other hand, I would put the Fox's news division operation against anybody's in terms of its overall genuine balance and fairness. When a viewer watches Shepard Smith, Bret Baier, or any of the correspondents on the channel's straight newscasts, the information might be presented in an edgy way, but not with an ideological bias. There is an extraordinary camaraderie, not only among the on-air personalities but also among the crews and staffs of the various shows. This is the result of an esprit de corps that would be unusual in any corporate environment but is especially noteworthy in the media world. I consider myself very fortunate to work among very talented, hardworking, and dedicated professionals who never resent a colleague's success but understand that the more successful any Fox show is, the better for all of us.

Of course, working on my own show has afforded me two unique opportunities: First, it has allowed me to continue to engage in discussion of policy issues that are very important to me and has given me a platform for sharing opinions and ideas. Second, I've been given the rewarding opportunity to meet some influential newsmakers as well as the biggest names in entertainment and music.

By the way, Fox executives were not sure, in the beginning, that the music feature of my show would be well received or work in that context. I held my ground, pushing hard to include music; today it is one of the most popular features, whether it's the music of our house band, "the little rockers"—made up of full-time Fox employees who range from cameramen to lighting technicians—or guest appearances by celebrity entertainers ranging from Willie Nelson to Neil Sedaka to George Jones, from Andy Williams to Lynyrd Skynyrd. People often come up to me in airports, in hotels, or on the street to tell me that it looks like I'm having a lot of fun playing my bass guitar with Meat Loaf, Toby Keith, or Tanya Tucker. I'm quick to tell them I'm having far more fun than I deserve. (I'm not sure I want Roger Ailes to know this, but there are days when I'd probably pay him for the opportunity to make music with some of the artists whom I grew up idolizing and seeking to emulate.)

One major part of my life for the past few years has been the pleasure of writing—a task I enjoy greatly, especially when I have time for it! Once a person writes a book, the other side of the process is marketing it through extensive book tours. For example, the December 2009 tour for my Christmas book, *A Simple Christmas*, had me on a bus for twenty-one consecutive days visiting sixty-four cities and signing well over fifty thousand copies. The hours are long and the schedule beyond grueling. To keep some level of sanity on the tour, my road crew and I started making notes of some of the wonderfully funny things people would say after standing in line (sometimes for up to four hours) in order to walk quickly up to the signing table, where I would extend a handshake and sign an autograph before having to turn to the next person. I was always amazed when as many as 1,400 people lined up for a signing, even though they knew that the total time they'd have to visit with me would be measured in seconds.

But some of them certainly took the opportunity to make an impression. A lady in Oklahoma leaned over the table and said, "Honey, I want you to know I've never waited this long on a man." In Kentucky, another lady said, "This is the most excited I've been since my wedding day." Then there was the Tennessee lady who announced, with a great deal of pride, "I want you to know that I shaved my legs for you today." (No, I had no intention of looking or feeling to see if she was telling the truth.) My crew helped put together a "quote of the day"—yes, these all made the cut—which we would discuss as we boarded the bus for the next stop, eating yet another meal on the road.

So this is my life today: busy, challenging, fascinating. As a reader, listener, or viewer, you and millions like you certainly play an important part in all of it. I try every day to keep in touch with the concerns of the American people. If you ever decide to help me in that goal by writing a letter or e-mailing me, pro or con, I can promise you will certainly be heard. Meanwhile, we all have a lot of work to do on maintaining those boundary stones. I hope some of the ideas I've discussed here will be helpful to that effort.

EPILOGUE

A Simple Election

In February of 1812, a cataclysmic earthquake struck near New Madrid, Missouri, with such seismic force that it caused the Mississippi River to flow backward for a time. Almost two hundred years later, scientists fear that this fault line poses the most significant threat for another massive earthquake, which could potentially devastate St. Louis and Memphis and cut off land transportation between the eastern and western halves of the United States.

On November 2, 2010, I witnessed another major seismic shift, one that spread throughout the country and changed the course of history. As I watched the results of election day come in, I was struck by how dramatically our country had changed in just a couple of years. No longer enamored with Obama's promise of "hope and change," voters turned over 63 seats in the U.S. House of Representatives (as of this writing 6 seats are still unconfirmed) and 7 seats in the U.S. Senate to the GOP. At the state level, a stunning 680 seats changed hands, dwarfing the 1994 election upheaval, which saw 472 seats ceded to Republicans.

Just two years ago, the Republican Party was said to be on its last leg, and pundits were not discussing *if* it would survive but how long before it would shrivel into a small and irrelevant political body. Not only is this a testament to how resilient the GOP has become, but it's also a testament to how volatile and fluid the political playing field really is. Right now we have reason to celebrate, but Republicans who were dancing into the night and feeling a new "pep in their step" had best be mindful that as easily as they were swept in they can be swept out.

Take a lesson from the Democrats. Their biggest mistake—as exemplified by the actions of Barack Obama, Nancy Pelosi, and Harry Reid—was to misread the election results of 2008 as a mandate to radically "transform" everything in sight—for better or worse. Americans aren't that keen on abrupt turns and radical overnight changes, and the Founders wisely designed our system to protect it from the whims of the moment or the many. My bass boat is nimble in the water and can turn on a dime even at high speeds, but an aircraft carrier requires miles of planning to make a 180-degree turn.

The 2010 election was a kick in the rear to the arrogant Congress that passed 2,300-page bills they hadn't read, spent trillions bailing out bad businesses, and threw taxpayer-funded life preservers to government employees and union workers while the economy sank and pulled small businesses down with it.

I spend a lot of time talking to voters—from all over the country and both sides of the fence—and I've found that people actually want much less from their government than politicians think. They want the trash picked up on time, smooth roads and safe streets, good schools, a fire truck to show up promptly when needed, and secure borders to keep bad people from getting in and disturbing our peace. They want veterans to be cared for, sick people, children, and old people to be treated decently, and laws to be enforced. That's about it. They don't need a "supernanny" telling them what to wear, what to eat, and how many hours of sleep to get each night. They don't want to work hard and then get penalized for their productivity so that government can reward the slackers and the failures. Americans simply don't buy the "everyone gets a trophy" socialist nonsense that has become all too pervasive in our culture of political correctness.

As I write this, just a few days after the election, the focus has already turned to 2012. This is the part of politics that I find most irksome—that we never stop playing the "game" of who's on top, who's climbing, and who's falling. The focus will soon be on money raised and machinery employed—instead of on ideas and policy innovations. The pundits will create their own biased and cynical scenarios, in which they will "create" front-runners by their perceptions based on the size of the war chests that candidates amass. They will begin to handicap the possible candidates based on what kinds of negative narratives are likely to be launched by political opponents or, in many cases, the media. I actually dread the process, having been through it before and contemplating whether to enter it again. There will be days on end of breathless news alerts that will "break" some big headline that a candidate made a C in a college math course or that a photo has surfaced showing a candidate in a ridiculous Halloween costume when he was sixteen.

America will be looking for a thoughtful, mature, seasoned, and tempered leader, but that search will likely be lost in a sea of "gotcha" games while political hacks and media hit men look for the slightest aberration in a candidate's history. It will be like having an extreme close-up in high definition to examine each freckle, while failing to notice whether the person is even wearing pants.

Let's hope that both political parties will do some serious growing up beyond the towel-popping pranks of legislative maneuvering and attempt to seriously address why we're losing jobs, slipping behind in world prestige, and having to be electronically strip-searched to get on an airplane because we haven't figured out how to rid ourselves of jihadism and terrorism.

As you finish this book (and, I hope, share it with others), I'd encourage you not to get too excited about the "hot" issues and potential candidates that are getting all the attention right now. If you think you know who the personalities and issues that will be that decide the 2012 election, just remember that four years ago, the "experts" assumed that Rudy Giuliani and Hillary Clinton would be the nominees for their parties and the deciding issue would be the war in Iraq. Who would have thought that John McCain and a guy with a strange name like Barack Obama would joust for the White House and that the main issue would be the economy?

Instead, focus on how we can genuinely resolve the ongoing challenges of our generation by applying some simple, commonsense principles to the complex and confusing issues that dominate the headlines. When I originally set out to write this book, I didn't intend for it to be a campaign book or a slam against the Democrats—and I hope you haven't read it that way. Although I've never hidden my political persuasion, I don't articulate a certain set of beliefs because I'm a party man, have an ax to grind, or want to be a part of the winning team. Of course, I'm as giddy as a schoolboy at the results of the recent election, but the only way to fix our country is to set aside our differences, stop the attack ads, and fully commit to doing what is best for America and the American people.

It's just that simple.

Acknowledgments

Despite the title of this book, the task of presenting "a simple government" wasn't so simple! In addition to attempting to distill many of the major issues America faces down to the simple principles that should be applied to confront them, I had to do thorough research to ensure that the book was accurate and sufficiently supported as well as thought provoking.

Thus, I'm indebted to many people without whose assistance I could not have completed the task on time. Janis Cherry, who served as my senior policy adviser during my presidential campaign, remains a trusted adviser and was very helpful in digging up great information for use in the book.

Pat and Laura Reeder work with me on a daily basis to help prepare the *Huckabee Report*, my radio commentary, which airs on nearly six hundred radio stations three times a day, five days a week, and were crucial in unearthing great stories and adding their unique touch. De-Wayne Hayes worked for me when I held the offices of lieutenant governor and governor before moving to Phoenix for a corporate writing gig and later enrolling in the advanced graduate study program for writers at Dartmouth. He was also vitally helpful in the latter stages of the project. Charles Flowers assisted in making sure the final manuscript was arranged in the most logical way.

I am forever grateful for the team at Sentinel for their support, encouragement, and sometimes gentle prodding to get the project brought in on time. I'm grateful for the very focused marketing team at Premiere Authors, who coordinated the grueling schedule of the book tour, because while utterly exhausting, the tour gives me the wonderful joy of meeting thousands of the good people who buy and read the book and allows me to say "thank you" in person.

As always, I am eternally grateful to my wife, Janet, my three adult children, and their spouses for their patience while I was out of touch writing and even more out of touch while on the road signing copies of the book. And, of course, I'm grateful for our three dogs, who missed me almost as much as I missed them but always made me laugh and kept my blood pressure normal.

My heartfelt thanks to them, but most of all to you for taking the time to read this book and, I hope, sharing its message with your friends and family.

Notes

CHAPTER ONE: The Most Important Form of Government Is a Father, a Mother, and Children

9   **"American innovation":** Barack Obama, "Remarks at West Point Graduation," West Point, New York (May 22, 2010).

9   **"The family has always been the cornerstone":** Ronald Reagan, "Abortion and the Conscience of the Nation," *National Review*, spring 1983.

10   **the Bolsheviks hated the institution:** a woman resident in Russia, "The Russian Effort to Abolish Marriage," *Atlantic Monthly*, July 1926.

12   **sent home for wearing an American flag T-shirt:** Joshua Rhett Miller, "California Students Sent Home for Wearing U.S. Flags on Cinco de Mayo," www.FOXNews.com, May 6, 2010.

13   **results of a CASA report:** "The Importance of Family Dinners V," National Center on Addiction and Substance Abuse at Columbia University, September 2009.

15   **"The disappearance of marriage":** Robert Rector, "Understanding Illegitimacy," *National Review*, April 12, 2010.

15   **one in three American kids:** "The Father Factor," National Fatherhood Initiative (available at www.fatherhood.org).

15   **These kids are five times:** http://www.fatherhood.org/Page.aspx?pid=403.

15   **"[L]iberal politicians . . . have a vested":** Robert Rector, "Understanding Illegitimacy," *National Review*, April 12, 2010.

16   **He is clearly dismayed to report:** Daniel Patrick Moynihan, "The Negro

Family: The Case for National Action," Office of Policy Planning and Research, United States Department of Labor, March 1965.

17 **As compiled by the Guttmacher Institute:** "Data Center," Guttmacher Institute (available at www.guttmacher.org/datacenter/index.jsp).

18 **"Grief still treads upon the heels of pleasure":** William Congreve, *The Old Bachelor*, 1693.

21 **Winston Churchill:** http://thinkexist.com/quotation/there_is_no_doubt_ that_it_is_around_the_family/161333.html.

22 **"Their grief, after nearly a year and a half":** Bob Herbert, "Bloody Urban Landscapes," *New York Times*, May 7, 2010.

CHAPTER TWO: The Further You Drift from Shore, the More Likely You Are to Be Lost at Sea

29 **"The powers delegated":** James Madison, "Number 45," *The Federalist Papers*, 1787–88.

29 **"All of us need to be reminded":** Ronald Reagan, "Inaugural Address" (Washington, DC, January 20, 1981).

30 **"Our citizens feel they've lost control":** Ronald Reagan, "State of the Union Address" (Washington, DC, January 26, 1982).

30 **"Joint state-federal spending":** Sven R. Larson, "Federal Funds and State Fiscal Independence," Heritage Foundation, May 15, 2008.

32 **"It is one of the happy":** Louis Brandeis, dissent, *New State Ice Co. v. Liebmann*, 285 U.S. 262 (1932).

34 **"More than five years ago":** Lawrence Wasden, "Federalism and America's Financial Crisis," *American Thinker*, April 3, 2009 (available at www.american thinker.com/2009/04/federalism_and_americas_finac.html).

37 **"spent more time fighting":** Bill Nungesser, quoted by Jim Efstathiou Jr., "Gulf Cleanup of BP Oil Foiled by Leadership Confusion," *Bloomberg BusinessWeek*, June 10, 2010.

CHAPTER THREE: You Can't Spend What You Don't Have; You Can't Borrow What You Can't Pay Back

41 **the Web site PageTutor.com:** "What Does One TRILLION Dollars *Look* Like?" *PageTutor.com* (available at www.pagetutor.comtrillion/index.html).

45 **"As we peer into society's future":** Dwight D. Eisenhower, "Farewell Address to the Nation," the White House, Washington, DC (January 17, 1961).

46 **"The consequences arising":** John Adams, "State of the Union Address," Philadelphia (November 11, 1797).

47 **"The Obama 10-year budget":** Michael Boskin, "When Deficits Become Dangerous," *Wall Street Journal*, February 11, 2010.

50 **according to an estimate by:** "The Long-Term Budget Outlook," Congressional Budget Office, June 2010.

55 **all of the approximately forty million:** Robert W. Fiarlie, "The Kauffman

Index of Entrepreneurial Activity, 1996–2009," May 2010, Kaufman Foundation of Entrepreneurship, http://www.kauffman.org/uploadedfiles/kiea_2010_report.pdf.

CHAPTER FOUR: If You Drain the Lake, All the Fish Will Die

63 **small businesses will have a 1,250 percent:** "New Law Increases Paperwork for Self-Employed Over a Thousand Percent," National Association for the Self-Employed, May 25, 2010.

63 **"Changes in marginal income tax rates":** Veronique de Rugy, "1920s Income Tax Cuts Sparked Economic Growth and Raised Federal Revenues," CATO Institute, March 4, 2003 (available at www.cato.org).

64 **Art Laffer, an economic adviser:** Arthur Laffer, "Tax Hikes and the 2011 Economic Collapse," *Wall Street Journal*, June 6, 2010.

64 **Scott Davis, the CEO of UPS:** Scott Davis, "Capital Gains Taxes and the Recovery," *Wall Street Journal*, June 4, 2010.

66 **Nicole Gelinas of the Manhattan Institute notes:** Nicole Gelinas, "How 'Soaking the Rich' Clobbers You," *New York Post*, April 14, 2010.

67 **"Reducing or eliminating the corporate tax":** Michael J. Boskin, "Time to Junk the Corporate Tax," *Wall Street Journal*, May 6, 2010.

67 **The U.S. statutory corporate tax rate:** Duanjie Chen and Jack Mintz, "U.S. Effective Corporate Tax Rate on New Investments: Highest in the OECD," *CATO Institute Tax & Budget Bulletin*, May 2010.

69 **"most harmful for growth":** Asa Johansson, Christopher Heady, Jens Arnold, Bert Brys, and Laura Vartia, "Tax and Economic Growth," *OECD Economics Department Working Papers*, July 11, 2008.

70 **cost $230 billion in 2009:** "Monthly Budget Review, Fiscal Year 2009," Congressional Budget Office, November 6, 2009.

70 **the areas that suffered the least:** Richard Florida, "Homeownership Is Overrated," *Wall Street Journal*, June 7, 2010.

71 **It's estimated that his estate:** Peter Whoriskey, "Steinbrenner Heirs Could Save Millions from the One-Year Gap in Estate Tax," *Washington Post*, July 14, 2010.

72 **eliminating the estate tax would create:** William Beach, "Now Is the Time to Permanently Repeal Federal Death Taxes," Heritage Foundation, June 16, 2003 (available at www.heritage.org).

CHAPTER FIVE: Once Humpty Dumpty Falls, It's Hard to
Put Him Back Together

75 **I know all too well about the dangers:** Mike Huckabee, *Quit Digging Your Grave with a Knife and Fork* (New York: Center Street, 2005).

76 **almost 30 percent of our health-care costs:** Larry R. Gettman, "Economic Benefits of Physical Activity," *President's Council on Physical Fitness and Sports Research Digest*, September 1996.

77 **"By our calculation, if the nation":** Steven A. Burd, "How Safeway Is Cutting Health-Care Costs," *Wall Street Journal,* June 12, 2009.

77 **Boeing has reduced:** http://www.bizjournals.com/seattle/stories/2010/04/26/story4.html.

78 **Obesity rates:** National Governor Association Best Practices Center; http://www.reuters.com/article/idUSTRE56Q36020090727.

78 **Obesity-related health-care costs:** National Governor Association Best Practices Center; http://www.reuters.com/article/idUSTRE56Q36020090727.

78 **on-the-job injuries were seven times higher:** "Obesity Increases Workers' Compensation Costs," Duke Medicine News and Communications, April 23, 2007 (available at www.DukeHealth.org).

78 **In addition to diabetes:** "'Beer Belly' Linked to Alzheimer's Disease," BBC News, May 20, 2010 (available at www.news.bbc.co.uk/2/hi/8693947.stm).

78 **Obesity is especially dangerous:** "Growing Obesity Increases Perils of Childbearing," New York Times, June 5, 2010; Anemona Hartocollis "Mothers' Obesity Tied to Newborn Heart Defects," Reuters, April 28, 2010.

79 **higher rates of Cesarean births:** *New York Times,* http://www.nytimes.com/2010/06/06/health/06obese.html.

79 **The babies of obese mothers:** http://www.reuters.com/article/idUSTRE63R4NH20100428.

79 **an obese woman who had a stroke:** Anemona Hartocollis, "Growing Obesity Increases Perils of Childbearing," *New York Times,* June 5, 2010.

80 **Since 1980:** National Governor Association Best Practices Center, http://healthyamericans.org/reports/obesity2009/.

80 **over 40 percent of parents with obese children:** "Parental Concerns About Childhood Obesity: Time for a Reality Check?" C.S. Mott Children's Hospital National Poll on Children's Health, December 10, 2007.

80 **Oregon has the lowest percentage of obese children:** Anne Harding, "Mississippi Has Most Obese Kids; Oregon Has the Least," Reuters, May 3, 2010.

80 **three recommendations for reducing childhood obesity:** Misti Crane, "Study: Family Routines Cut the Risk of Childhood Obesity," *Columbus Dispatch,* February 8, 2010.

81 **It's even having an impact on the military:** "Too Fat to Fight: Retired Military Leaders Want Junk Food Out of America's Schools," Mission: Readiness, April 20, 2010.

84 **"No one but Mr. Romney disagrees":** Joseph Rago, "The Massachusetts Health-Care 'Train Wreck,'" *Wall Street Journal,* July 7, 2010.

85 **"will soon have affordable health insurance":** Mitt Romney, "Health Care for Everyone?" *Wall Street Journal,* April 11, 2006.

85 **Massachusetts Taxpayers Foundation stepped into the lab:** Robert J. Samuelson, "As Massachusetts Health 'Reform' Goes, So Could Go Obamacare," *Washington Post,* July 19, 2010.

85 **premiums in Massachusetts under RomneyCare are rising:** Joan Vennochi, "The Forbidding Arithmetic of Healthcare Reform," *Boston Globe,* June 28, 2009.

86 **"The decision is not whether or not we will ration care":** Dr. Donald Berwick, quoted by Katherine T. Adams, "Rethinking Comparative Effectiveness Research," Biotechnology Healthcare, June 2009, 6(2): 35–36, 38.

87 **"Limited resources require decisions":** Donald Berwick, "A Shared Statement of Ethical Principles for Those Who Shape and Give Health Care," *Annals of Internal Medicine*, January 19, 1999, vol. 130 no. 2, 143–47.

CHAPTER SIX: If You Don't Hear the School Bell Ring, Class Never Starts

90 **Yet about one-third:** Jason Amos, "Dropouts, Diplomas, and Dollars: U.S. High Schools and the Nation's Economy," Alliance for Excellent Education, August 2008.

91 **A dropout can expect to earn:** Ibid.

91 **At City College of San Francisco:** David Moltz, "Competing Principles," Inside Higher Ed, June 28, 2010 (available at www.insidehighered.com/news/2010/06/28/remediation).

92 **$25,000 median income:** http://nces.ed.gov/fastfacts/display.asp?id=77.

93 **initial group of students:** op-ed by Adam B. Schaeffer, "Florida's Unheralded School Revolution," *Wall Street Journal*, May 1, 2010.

93 **the results of national reading tests:** Sam Dillon, "Stagnant National Reading Scores Lag Behind Math," *New York Times*, March 24, 2010.

94 **There are more than five thousand:** Number of US Charter Schools Grows by 9 percent in 2010," Center for Education Reform, http://www.edreform.com/Home/?Number_of_US_Charter_Schools_Grows_By_9_Percent_in_2010, accessed November 13, 2010. (http://www.uscharterschools.org), last updated February 28, 2010.

94 **A 2009 study by Margaret Raymond:** Margaret Raymond, "Multiple Choice: Charter School Performance in 16 States," Stanford University, 2009.

95 **"As a former teacher":** Timothy Knowles, "The Trouble with Teacher Tenure," *Wall Street Journal*, June 18, 2010.

96 **"When I first came here ":** Michelle Rhee, quoted by Stephen Brill, "The Teachers' Unions' Last Stand," *New York Times Magazine*, May 17, 2010.

96 **While more than half the states:** Stuart Buck and Jay P. Greene, "Blocking, Diluting, and Co-Opting Merit Pay" (presented at PEPG Conference: Merit Pay: Will It Work? Is It Politically Viable?, Harvard University, Cambridge, MA, June 2010).

98 **Supreme Court of Arkansas:** http://www.schoolfunding.info/states/ar/11-21-02supremecourt.php3.

Notes

CHAPTER SEVEN: Leave Your Campsite in Better Shape Than You Found It

105 **one story in particular:** Theodore Roosevelt, *Theodore Roosevelt: An Autobiography* (New York: Macmillan Company, 1913), 17–18.

107 **Lyndon Johnson once put it:** http://www.brainyquote.com/quotes/quotes/l/lyndonbjo144728.html.

108 **"To waste":** http://www.pbs.org/weta/thewest/resources/archives/eight/trcon serv.htm.

108 **"What is a conservative but one":** Ronald Reagan, "Remarks at Dedication of National Geographic Society New Headquarters Building" (June 19, 1984).

108 **"Man is treated as if he were":** Ayn Rand, *Return of the Primitive: The Anti-Industrial Revolution* (New York: Plume, 1999), 277.

109 **some 60 percent of us live:** American Lung Association, "New American Lung Association Report Finds 60 Percent of Americans Live in Areas Where Air Is Dirty Enough to Endanger Lives," April 29, 2009 (available at www.lungusa.org/press-room/press-releases/10th-annual-state-of-the-air.html).

111 **worrisome emissions:** http://en.wikipedia.org/wiki/Electricity_generation.

111 **about 70 percent of our states have renewable:** U.S. Department of Energy, "States with Renewable Portfolio Standards," May 2009 (available at www.appsl.eere.energy.gov/states/maps/renewable_portfolio_states.cfm).

111 **clever little gizmos:** http://www.srpnet.com/newsroom/releases/051810.aspx.

111 **Only about one in ten American households:** Steve Hargreaves, "Millions of Homes to Get Smart Meters," www.CNNMoney.com, October 27, 2009.

113 **If, as the Department of Energy predicts:** Joel Kirkland and Climatewire, "Global Emissions Predicted to Grow Through 2035," *Scientific American*, May 26, 2010.

113 **"Expanding nuclear energy makes both environmental":** Christine Todd Whitman, "The Case for Nuclear Power," *Bloomberg BusinessWeek*, September 17, 2007.

115 **burning the city's nonrecyclable garbage:** Norman Steisel and Benjamin Miller, "Power from Trash," *New York Times*, April 27, 2010.

115 **almost 350,000 households:** op-ed by Rose George, ". . . And Sewage, Too," *New York Times*, April 28, 2010. The article says 340,000 households, which I rounded to "almost 350,000," and it says 430,000 cars, which I rounded to "almost half a million."

115 **"The role of government":** http://quotationsbook.com/quote/45475/.

116 **The Minerals Management Service (MMS):** Patrick Jonsson, "Gulf Oil Spill: Is MMS So Corrupt It Must Be Abolished?" *Christian Science Monitor*, May 26, 2010.

117 **According to Thad Allen, whom Obama:** Jennifer Lebovich and Carol Rosenberg, "Oil Seeps into Florida Waterways," *Miami Herald*, January 11, 2010.

118 **"Never let a serious crisis go to waste":** Rahm Emanuel, quoted by Jeff Zeleny, "Obama Weighs Quick Undoing of Bush Policy," *New York Times*, November 9, 2008.

119 **That's exactly what I did:** Thomas L. Friedman, "We're Gonna Be Sorry," *New York Times*, July 24, 2010.

122 five-trillion-dollar market: "Captains of Subsidy," *Wall Street Journal*, June 16, 2010.

122 sixty thousand barrels of oil: Mark P. Mills, "Notes from Underground," *Wall Street Journal*, July 2, 2010.

122 At nineteen million barrels a day: CIA World Factbook, https://www.ccia .gov/library/publications/the-world-factbook/rankorder/2174rank.html; Spencer Swartz and Shai Oster, "China Tops U. S. in Energy," *Wall Street Journal*, July 20, 2010.

123 "There are many guesses as to what": Stuart Butler and Kim R. Holmes, "Twelve Principles to Guide U.S. Energy Policy," Heritage Foundation, June 26, 2007.

124 "There is little doubt that China's growing": David Pumphrey, quoted by Spencer Swartz and Shai Oster, "China Tops U.S. in Energy Use," *Wall Street Journal*, July 18, 2010.

125 This milestone: http://online.wsj.com/article/SB1000142405274870372050 45 75376712353150310.html.

126 "These efforts to dominate renewable energy": Keith Bradsher, "China Leading Global Race to Make Clean Energy," *New York Times*, January 30, 2010.

126 In 1999, the country produced: http://www.nytimes.com/2010/01/31/business/ energy-environment/31renew.html; http://www.nytimes.com/2010/09/09/busi ness/global/09trade.html.

127 "OPEC sets oil's price ": R. James Woolsey, "How to End America's Addiction to Oil," *Wall Street Journal*, April 15, 2010.

127 the projection of American gas reserves: http://www.naturalgas.org/ overview/resources.asp.

128 For all of these reasons: Matthew L. Wald, "Study Says Natural Gas Use Likely to Double," *New York Times*, June 25, 2010.

CHAPTER EIGHT: Good Fences Make Good Neighbors

132 almost half of Silicon Valley's: http://www.dukenews.duke.edu/2007/01/ engineerstudy.html.

132 "We cannot build a unified country": George W. Bush, "Address to the Nation on Immigration Reform," the White House, Washington, DC (May 15, 2006).

133 case Tom Brokaw documented of a family: Tom Brokaw, "The 21st Century Immigrant Story," NBC News, December 27, 2006.

133 "If we didn't have immigrant labor": Thomas Green, quoted by Christopher Helman, "Labor Pains," *Forbes*, June 28, 2010.

134 "Unfortunately, reform has been held": Barack Obama, "Remarks on Immigration," American University, Washington, DC (July 1, 2010).

135 But it pushed the same poison: Charles E. Schumer and Lindsey O. Graham, "The Right Way to Mend Immigration," *Washington Post*, March 19, 2010.

135 comprehensive immigration reform: http://www.foxnews.com/politics/ 2010/06/21/kyl-obama-wont-secure-border-lawmakers-immigrationpackage/.

Notes

"have been more than patient": Jan Brewer, quoted by Peter Slevin, "Both Sides in Immigration Debate Blame Congressional Inaction for Arizona Law," *Washington Post*, April 27, 2010.

136 **"completely unacceptable":** Gabrielle Giffords, "Giffords: Bipartisanship on Border Security Is Possible," www.giffords.house.gov, October 13, 2010.

137 **"Our failure to act":** http://www.politico.com/politico44/perm/0410/w_h_watching_arizona_ae7a3dff-98b5-40e2-a702-1eacf15518e1.html.

137 **2010 National Drug Control Strategy:** Office of National Drug Control Policy, "2010 National Strategy," October 30, 2010 (available at www.white housedrugpolicy.gov/strategy/).

137 **The 2009 National Survey of Drug Use:** http://www.oas.samhsa.gov/NSDUH/2k9NSDUH/2k9Results.htm#1.1.

138 **they'd not bothered to actually read:** "Napolitano Admits She Hasn't Read Arizona Immigration Law in 'Detail,'" www.FOXNews.com, May 18, 2010.

138 **"a misdirected expression of frustration":** Barack Obama, quoted by Jonathan Weisman, "Obama Gets an Earful from Mexico's Calderón," *Wall Street Journal*, May 19, 2010.

139 **Assistant Secretary of State Michael Posner:** Kirit Radia, "US Cites AZ Immigration Law During Human Rights Talks with China, Conservatives Call It an Apology," ABC News, May 17, 2010.

139 **"The Mexican government condemns the approval":** Jonathan J. Cooper, "Arizona Immigration Law Target of Protest," Associated Press, April 26, 2010.

139 **In fact, a recent *New York Times*/CBS News poll:** Randal C. Archibold and Megan Thee-Brenan, "Poll Shows Most in U.S. Want Overhaul of Immigration Laws," *New York Times*, May 3, 2010.

141 **workplace arrests:** http://www.foxnews.com/politics/2010/08/23/company-audits-illegal-worker-arrests-way/.

141 **About 60 percent of illegals:** Hans von Spakovsky, "A Broken Immigration Court System," Heritage Foundation, June 18, 2010. He says 59 percent don't show up; I rounded that up to say "about 60 percent." He says that "only 9 percent" appeal; I said that "almost 90 percent . . . don't appeal."

141 **1.2 million illegal Mexican immigrants went home:** Stephen A. Camorota and Karen Jensenius, "A Shifting Tide: Recent Trends in the Illegal Immigrant Population," Center for Immigration Studies, July 2009.

141 **Mexican immigration in 2008–9 was one-fourth:** Jeffrey S. Passel and D'Vera Cohn, "Mexican Immigrants: How Many Come? How Many Leave?" Pew Hispanic Center, July 22, 2009.

142 **immigrants started one-quarter of all new:** Kauffman Foundation, "America's Loss Is the World's Gain: America's New Immigrant Entrepreneurs, Part IV," March 2009.

142 **"except of useful mechanics":** http://www.humanevents.com/article.php?id=21626.

142 **Hispanic students remain:** http://www.cis.org/california-education.

142 **illegal immigration costs all of us $113 billion:** Jack Martin, "The Fiscal Burden of Illegal Immigration on U.S. Taxpayers," Federation for American Immigration Reform, July 2010.

CHAPTER NINE: Bullies on the Playground Understand Only One Thing

145   **it was Rick Rescorla:** Amanda Ripley, "A Survival Guide to Catastrophe," *Time*, May 29, 2008.

148   **the president spoke at the Fort Hood:** Barack Obama, "Remarks by the President at Memorial Service at Fort Hood," Fort Hood, Texas (November 10, 2009).

148   **excerpt from the congressional hearing:** Eric Holder, testimony before House Judiciary Committee, Oversight of the U.S. Department of Justice, May 13, 2010, http://judiciary.house.gov/hearings/pdf/Holder100513.pdf.

149   **"I don't know why":** http://www.washingtontimes.com/news/2010/may/14/holder-balks-at-blaming-radical-islam/.

150   **"A Muslim has no nationality except his belief":** Sayyid Qutb, "A Muslim's Nationality and His Belief."

151   **"jihad against America is binding upon myself":** Anwar al-Awlaki, quoted by Cynthia Johnson, "Yemen Preacher Urges Jihad on United States: Tape," Reuters, March 18, 2010.

151   **"one of its own citizens far from a combat zone":** Scott Shane, "U.S. Approval of Killing of Cleric Causes Unease," *New York Times*, May 13, 2010.

151   **"Must I shoot":** http://en.wikipedia.org/wiki/The_Constitution_is_not_a_suicide_pact.

152   **"If the court does not temper":** Robert Jackson, dissent, *Terminiello v. City of Chicago*, 337 U.S. 1 (1949).

154   **"an unnecessarily protracted, risk-averse process":** Ray Kelly, quoted in "Ray Kelly's Wiretap Alarm," *Wall Street Journal*, December 8, 2008.

154   **"We didn't know they had progressed":** John Brennan, "Briefing by Homeland Security Secretary Napolitano, Assistant to the President for Counterterrorism and Homeland Security Brennan, and Press Secretary Gibbs," Washington, DC (January 7, 2010).

157   **A man who bought a condo:** James Barron and Michael S. Schmidt, "From Suburban Father to a Terrorism Suspect," *New York Times*, May 4, 2010.

157   **the unclassified summary of a report:** Senate Select Committee on Intelligence, "Unclassified Executive Summary of the Committee Report on the Attempted Terrorist Attack on Northwest Airlines Flight 253," 111th Congr., 2d sess., May 18, 2010.

160   **Charles Faddis has written, there is:** Charles S. Faddis, *Willful Neglect* (Guildford, CT: Lyons Press, 2010).

160   **Clarke predicts:** http://www.dailymail.co.uk/news/worldnews/article-1275001/U-S-prepare-cyber-attack-ruin-country-just-15-MINUTES-expert-warns.html.

162   **In a survey taken there in April 2010:** Richard A. Opel Jr. and Taimoor Shah, "A Killing Further Erodes Afghan Faith in Leaders," *New York Times*, April 20, 2010.

163   **"not an adequate partner":** Karl Eikenberry, quoted by Thomas L. Friedman, "This Time We Really Mean It," *New York Times*, March 30, 2010.

165   **"The ideology of global jihad":** Bruce Riedel, quoted by David E. Sanger,

"U.S. Pressure Helps Militants Overseas Focus Efforts," *New York Times*, May 8, 2010.

CHAPTER TEN: When the Bullets Are Real, There Aren't Any Toy Soldiers

169　**20 percent of Iraq and Afghanistan vets:** RAND, "Invisible Wounds: Mental Health and Cognitive Care Needs of America's Returning Veterans," 2008.

169　**Stanford University study concluded it was likely:** Allen G. Breed, "In Tide of PTSD Cases, Fear of Fraud Growing," Associated Press, May 3, 2010.

169　**Soldiers serving the multiple deployments:** Mary Susan Littlepage, "Multiple Deployments Lead to Major Increase in PTSD Cases, New Study Says," Truthout, January 5, 2010 (available at www.truth-out.org/105098).

169　**traumatic brain injury (TBI):** Iraq and Afghanistan Veterans of America 2010 Legislative Agenda, published in January 2010. The TBI stat is from page 14 (it says 19 percent, and I rounded that up to "almost 20 percent").

169　**Mental health problems:** Iraq and Afghanistan Veterans of America 2010 Legislative Agenda, published in January 2010. The mental health problems stat is from page 14 (it says "more than 227,000," and I rounded that up to "almost 250,000").

170　**the rate of foreclosure:** http://www.bloomberg.com/apps/news?pid=newsarchive&sid=awj2TMDLnwsU.

171　**about 130,000 of these men and women:** http://www.washingtontimes.com/news/2009/dec/06/bassuk-ending-homelessness-returning-war-veterans/.

172　**20 percent of its disability ratings:** Iraq and Afghanistan Veterans of America 2010 Legislative Agenda, published in January 2010. The 20 percent disability ratings stat is from page 4 (it says "about 17%," and I rounded that up to "almost 20 percent").

172　**"Our goal is to give them the best":** Joe Villalobos, quoted by Michelle Roberts, "New Program Rebuilds Faces of Soldiers, Vets," Associated Press, July 31, 2010.

177　**"military life is fundamentally":** http://www.law.cornell.edu/uscode/10/654.html.

178　**10 percent said they would leave:** Brendan McGarry, "Troops Oppose Repeal of 'Don't Ask,'" *Military Times*, December 29, 2008.

179　**48 percent of conservatives describe themselves:** John Fritze, "Poll: More Americans 'Extremely Patriotic,'" *USA Today*, July 2, 2010.

179　**discharges for homosexuality:** http://www.cmrlink.org/HMilitary.asp?docID=360.

CHAPTER ELEVEN: With Enemies Like This, Who Needs Friends?

182　**Obama's handpicked commander was even forced:** Michael Hastings, "The Stanley McChrystal Scoop that Changed History," *Rolling Stone*, July 8–22, 2010.

183 **Churchill has less happy connotations:** Tim Shipman, "Barack Obama Sends Bust of Winston Churchill on Its Way Back to Britain," *Daily Telegraph*, February 14, 2009.

184 **"Any world order that elevates one nation":** Barack Obama, "Remarks by the President on a New Beginning at Cairo University," Cairo, Egypt (June 4, 2009).

184 **"No one nation":** http://www.telegraph.co.uk/news/worldnews/northamerica/usa/barackobama/6231623/Barack-Obamas-vision-of-American-foreign-policy.html.

184 **"For we must consider":** http://www.historytools.org/sources/winthrop-charity.pdf.

184 **"I believe in American exceptionalism":** Barack Obama, "Remarks at the NATO Summit," Straasbourg, France (April 4, 2009).

185 **"Our long-term security will come not":** Toby Harnden, "Barack Obama Declares the 'War on Terror' Is Over," *Daily Telegraph*, May 27, 2010.

185 **"we are enhancing":** http://www.whitehouse.gov/sites/default/files/rss_viewer/national_security_strategy.pdf.

186 **"a tectonic rift":** http://www.guardian.co.uk/world/2010/jun/27/israel-us-relations-tectonic-rift.

186 **"Islam is not part of the problem":** Obama, "Remarks by the President on a New Beginning."

188 **"Settlements have to be stopped":** Barack Obama, "Remarks by President Obama and Prime Minister Netanyahu of Israel in Press Availability," Washington, DC (May 18, 2009).

189 **"does not accept the legitimacy":** "Obama: U.S. Does Not Recognize 'Legitimacy of Continued Israeli Settlements,'" www.FOXNews.com, September 23, 2009.

190 **"Let me be clear, this is not":** Barack Obama, "Remarks by the President at the United Nations Security Council Summit on Nuclear Non-Proliferation and Nuclear Disarmament," United Nations (September 24, 2009).

190 **it "deplores the decision to single out Israel":** Janine Zacharia and Mary Beth Sheridan, "Israel Angry Over Being Singled Out in Action Plan on Nuclear Weapons," *Washington Post*, May 30, 2010.

191 **"abandoned Israel in the U.N.":** Elliot Abrams, "Joining the Jackals," *Weekly Standard*, June 2, 2010.

191 **"to provide the time and the space":** Barack Obama, "Press Conference by President Obama, Russian President Medvedev," Washington, DC (June 24, 2010).

192 **"sensed desperation in the Obama administration":** John Bolton, quoted by Peter Baker and David E. Sanger, "U.S. Makes Concessions to Russia for Iran Sanctions," *New York Times*, May 21, 2010.

192 **"Let's not forget that Russia supported":** David J. Kramer, quoted by Peter Baker and David E. Sanger, "U.S. Makes Concessions to Russia for Iran Sanctions," *New York Times*, May 21, 2010.

192 **"Will it deter [Iran] from their ambitions":** Leon Panetta, quoted in "CIA Director Skeptical of Iran Sanctions," *Washington Times*, June 27, 2010.

192 **"America will always seek a world":** Barack Obama, "Remarks at West Point Graduation," West Point, NY (May 22, 2010).

EPILOGUE: A Simple Election

205 **63 seats in the U.S. House of Representatives:** http://elections.nytimes .com/2010/results/house; http://elections.nytimes.com/2010/results/senate.

Index

Index

Index

Schumer, Chuck, 135
Schwarzenegger, Arnold, 35
Self-government, benefits of, 25
September 11 attacks, 145–47, 149
Sewage problem, 115
Shahzad, Faisal, 148, 151, 155, 156–57, 164
Sheehan, Michael, 159
Simple Christmas, A, 203–4
Smart diplomacy, 181–82, 193
Smart meters, 110–12
Smith, Cameron, 72
Smith, Lamar, 148
Social safety net programs, 48–49
Social Security, 52–54
    funding source of, 53–54
    running out, 53
    solution to problems of, 53–54
Sorensen, Dr. Susanne, 78
State government
    education, responsibility for, 93–95, 98–99
    Founders' intentions for, 28–29, 38
    as laboratory for national government, 32–33
    neglect by federal, 36–37
    stimulus money refused by, 31
    unions, negative influence on, 35–36
Steinbrenner, George, 71
Steisel, Norm, 115
Stimulus money
    amount of, 30
    better alternative to, 50–51
    and federal control, 30–32
    refused by states, 31
Subprime mortgages, 33–35

Taliban, 161–64
Taxation, 61–73
    capital gains tax, 64–65, 68
    colonial revolt against, 61–62
    corporate tax rates, 67–68
    cuts, benefits of, 65–66
    estate tax, 71–72
    FairTax, 69–70
    forms/paperwork burden, 63
    homeownership breaks, 70–71
    incentives, danger of, 64
    increase under Obama, 66

nonincome tax states, 63
nonpayers, 56–57
raising, dangers of, 57, 68–69
raising and GDP, 57, 68
tiered system, 65
top taxpayers, 56
Tea Party movement, 196
Tenure, teachers, 95–98
Terrorism, 145–66
    Afghanistan war, 161–65
    cyberattacks, 160–61
    and Israel, 186–87, 191
    naming the enemy, neglect of, 148–50
    no-fly lists, 156–58
    and Obama administration, 147–48, 152–54, 159, 161, 164–65
    Pakistan-U.S. relations, 163–64
    and radical Islam, 148, 150–51, 153
    roots of, 150–52
    September 11 attacks, 145–47, 149
    underestimating enemy, 154–58
    U.S. counterterrorism departments, 153–54, 159–60
Treasury bonds, 51–52

Underwood, David, 167–68
Unions, negative influence of, 35–36
USS *Cole*, 149

Veterans, 167–80
    employment, 173–76
    health care, limitations of, 171–72
    homelessness, 170–71
    mental health problems of, 169–70
Veterans Employment Opportunities Act, 173
Villalobos, Dr. Joe, 172
Vouchers
    Medicare alternative, 54–55
    school, 93–94

Wasden, Lawrence, 34
Waste management, 114–15
Whitman, Christine Todd, 113
Wind power, 128–29
Winthrop, John, 184
Woolsey, James, 127
Wrigley, P. K., 71–72

228